the little book of quick fixes
for eco conscious cleaning

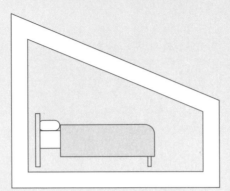

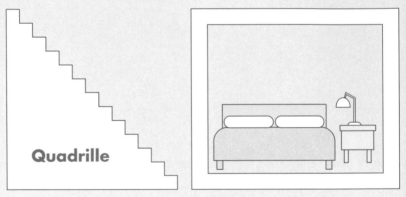

Quadrille

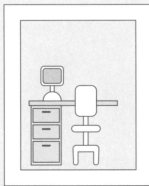

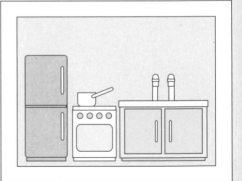

THE LITTLE BOOK OF

QUICK FIXES
FOR ECO CONSCIOUS
CLEANING

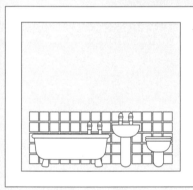

**Bridget
Bodoano**

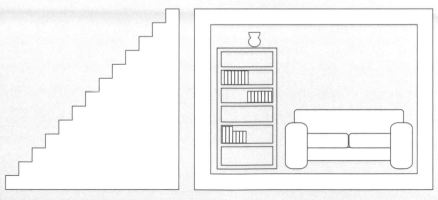

First published in 2006 by
Quadrille Publishing Ltd.
Alhambra House
27–31 Charing Cross Road
London WC2H 0LS

Editorial Director Jane O'Shea
Creative Director Helen Lewis
Project Editor Lisa Pendreigh
Designer Claire Peters
Illustrator Bridget Bodoano
Production Director Vincent Smith
Production Controller Bridget Fish

Cataloging in Publication Data: a catalogue record for this book
is available from the British Library.

ISBN: 978 184400 473 7

Printed in Singapore

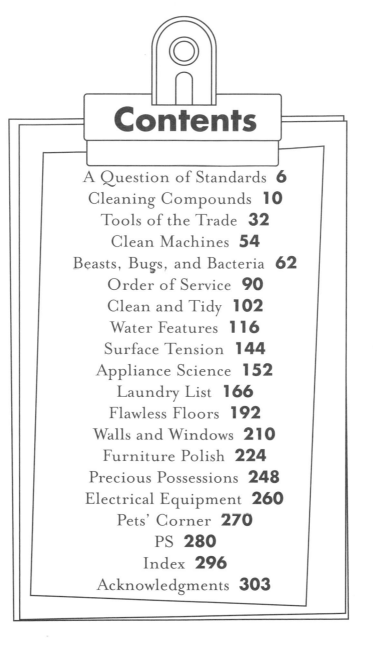

Contents

A Question Of Standards

how clean is clean?

On the whole, a clean home is a much nicer place to live for you and your family, partner, or housemates. Just how clean is clean depends on your own standards and character, but most of us fall into one of the following categories:

cleanaholic

Pristine perfectionists disinfect surfaces, empty the garbage, and clean sinks and bathtubs on a daily basis. They regularly indulge in thorough-cleaning routines, leaving no ornament unturned in their pursuit of dust control. They are also likely to treat ironing as a leisure activity.

clean enough

With less time—or better things to do—these perfectly normal people are more likely to do a good weekly clean rather than a daily clean. However, they clean up any obvious spills promptly. They will ignore the occassional cobweb, but like a clean floor.

slightly grubby

Not as tuned in to dirt and grime as others, the occupants of slightly grubby homes do what they think is basic cleaning, but only tackle what they see. They seldom venture into corners and underneath things, are generally dust-tolerant, and don't notice (or care about) a few small stains or dribbles.

complete slob

For reasons known only to themselves, they are oblivious to the fact that cleaning exists. Whether through a lack of education or self-esteem, they are happy to live in squalor until struck down by either conscience or a nasty infection.

Standard Requirements

Even those who think they keep a clean home are often in dirt-denial, so take off the rose-tinteds and have a good look around to check your credentials. If three or more of the following are present in your home, it is time to start cleaning:

- an excess of smears, splodges, and dribbles, plus rings from mugs and glasses
- more than a day's worth of dirty dishes in the kitchen
- more than one piece of moldy food
- black mold and mildew on walls, tiles, or floors
- nasty smells
- areas of unidentifiable stuff, which is gooey, greasy, or sticky
- obvious finger marks
- dust that has a greenish tinge
- large balls of dust
- a very dirty stovetop
- overflowing trash containers
- serious dirt around handles, especially on refrigerators
- dark brown stains in sinks, toilets, and bathtubs
- floors whose true color is difficult to determine

I Cleaning Compounds

Knowing a little of the chemistry of cleaning will help you choose the right products. Whether you opt for the old-fashioned simplicity of baking soda and vinegar, inexpensive proprietary brands, or their eco-friendly equivalents, the fact is that both daily maintenance and thorough cleaning can be carried out very effectively with a relatively small number of products.

Chemistry Lessons

soaps and detergents

Also known as surfactants, soaps and detergents assist in the wetting process by breaking down the surface tension of water, surrounding the dirt molecules and then preventing them from being reabsorbed. Soaps are made from animal or vegetable fats and oils whereas detergents are made from petrochemicals. Soap is not necessarily milder than detergent, but the fact that the latter are made from petrochemicals makes soap more eco-friendly. However, soap forms scum that can be a problem especially in hard-water areas.

solvents

The most common and gentle solvent is water; when mixed with soaps and detergents, water can dissolve most forms of dirt. More serious stains and dirt may need stronger solvents. Turpentine and mineral spirits are used in specialty cleaning products, but because they are potentially hazardous they should be used sparingly and carefully.

acids and alkalis

These do the job of dirt-busting. Their strength is measured in pH, indicated by a number from 0 to 14. Below pH 7 is considered acidic, pH 7 is neutral, and anything above is alkaline. The farther away from neutral they are, the harsher they are, especially on skin. Alkalis work well on grease or oily dirt, and so laundry products and kitchen cleaners tend to be alkaline. Acids are good at removing soap scum and hard-water deposits, so most bathroom cleaners are mildly acidic. Acids and alkalis neutralize one another so don't think that using strong forms of both will be doubly effective; in fact, they will cancel each other out.

Safety First

All cleaning products are potentially hazardous if they are used incorrectly, ingested, or come into contact with skin, so **BE WARNED.**

read labels

Labels contain important information regarding contents, instructions for use, safety warnings, and what to do in case of accidents.

follow instructions

Failure to use a product correctly can produce poor results as well as potential damage or a risk to health and safety.

keep safe

Keep all cleaning products out of the reach of children and away from food.

do not decant

Leave products in their original containers. As well as having access to the information on the label, you are at less risk of using the wrong product or mistaking it for something else.

use carefully

Strong cleaners often include toxic chemicals and solvents, such as alcohol, which are highly inflammable. Make sure they do not come in contact with skin, fabrics, carpets, and furniture.

use sparingly

Do not exceed stated doses. Using more doesn't necessarily mean a quicker or better result, although instructions on the label may suggest higher amounts in certain circumstances.

bleach alert

Never mix chlorine bleach with any other product. Combined with acids, alkalis, ammonia (and urine), chlorine creates chlorine gas... which kills.

Cleaning Basics

The sight of all those cleaning products on the supermarket shelves is enough to give anyone the vapors. But don't panic. The principles of getting things clean are pretty simple, and a few good basics are all you need. Look at the labels and choose those with the fewest and least scary-sounding ingredients, and the least number of warnings and conditions for use.

hand dishwashing liquid

A mild cleanser useful not only for doing the dishes but for many jobs, from cleaning worktops and paintwork to mopping the floor or removing stains from fabrics and furniture.

cream cleansers

These contain abrasives that help to remove dirt. The major brands are usually fairly gentle and can be safely used on most surfaces with a nonscratch sponge or cloth. For tough jobs, use with a scouring cloth or brush, but only on robust surfaces.

multipurpose cleaner

A multipurpose cleaning liquid with no abrasives can be used on all surfaces including sinks, bathtubs, and floors. It can be used neat or diluted in water.

chlorine bleach / disinfectant

Chlorine bleach is an effective germ-killer and will dissolve stains and whiten fabrics. When diluted it is safe to use in areas where food is prepared as a general disinfectant. Chlorine bleach is often the germ-killing ingredient in disinfectants, which work in much the same way as household bleach but are formulated for safe use for medicinal purposes. **Remember, don't mix chlorine bleach with any other cleaning materials.**

Cleaning Compounds

Green Issues

Concern for the planet and personal health has increased the popularity of eco-friendly cleaning products. Choose to be totally "green" or opt for a mix of eco and non-eco, where you are "green" most of the time but use stronger products for tough jobs.

standard cleaning products

FOR

- they are very effective
- they are fast-acting
- they are often less expensive than eco-alternatives

AGAINST

- they can contain highly toxic and corrosive chemicals
- the processes involved in their manufacture can cause pollution
- too many chemicals are being flushed into the water system causing pollution
- chemicals in cleaners are linked to allergic reactions, including asthma

eco-friendly products

• they use more environmentally friendly ingredients and production
• natural ingredients are biodegradable and therefore better for the sewage and water-supply systems
• they are safer and less toxic (although natural products can be dangerous in high doses)
• they are less likely to irritate skin and usually smell nice
• they are less likely to provoke allergic reactions

• some are less effective than standard equivalents
• they are usually more expensive than standard equivalents

Green Chemistry

You can concoct your own eco-friendly homemade cleansers from simple, inexpensive ingredients. Some are readily available in supermarkets or home-improvement stores, but you may have to ask for others at a drugstore or specialty store. They may not be quite as efficient as their modern, chemically laden alternatives so you may need to clean more frequently, allow more time for them to work, and use more elbow grease.

green chemistry set

- **soap** (surfactant)—eco-friendly dishwashing liquid
- **solvents**—water mostly, but use turpentine, mineral spirits, or eucalyptus oil for heavy-duty oil and grease
- **acids**—white vinegar, lemon juice, carbonated water
- **alkalis**—baking soda (sodium bicarbonate), borax, washing soda (sodium carbonate)
- **natural disinfectants**—white vinegar, lemon juice, tea-tree oil, eucalyptus oil

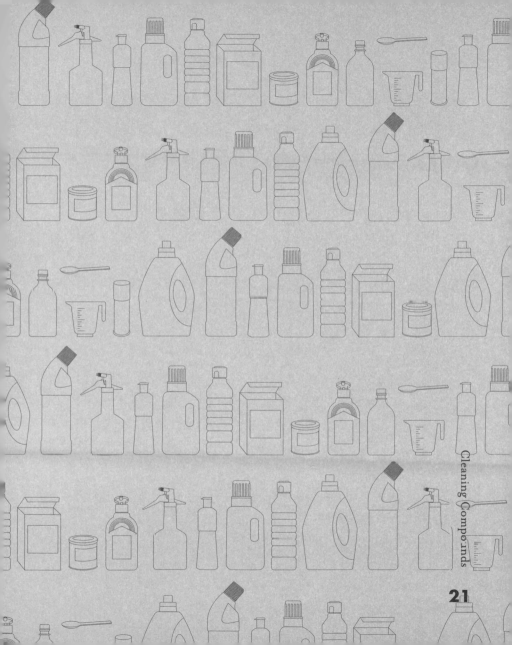

Green Ingredients

vinegar

Vinegar is the product of choice among the cleaning intelligentsia. It is an acid and is very versatile. As well as being a useful culinary ingredient, it's a good dirt buster and is brilliant for dissolving limescale. It is also a natural and very safe disinfectant. Any vinegar will perform these tasks but distilled white vinegar is best. It can be used undiluted for stains and tough limescale or diluted with water.

lemon juice

Lemon juice is an acid that cuts through grease. Fresh lemons are best and you can also use the squeezed halves to wipe over surfaces to clean and disinfect them.

baking soda
(sodium bicarbonate)

Readily available in supermarkets, baking soda is an alkali and a versatile cleaner. It can be used neat or dissolved in water or vinegar, and can be made into a paste. It reacts with water or vinegar to produce fizz to speed up the cleaning process.

borax

A nontoxic alkali available as a white crystaline powder, borax disinfects, bleaches, and deodorizes. It is also an effective insecticide and fungicide.

washing soda
(sodium carbonate)

A mild alkali sold in crystal form, washing soda can be used as a general cleaner, is a good stain remover, and is useful for unblocking waste pipes.

5 Simple Solutions

Despite the plethora of cleaning materials on the market these basic cleaning solutions are good enough for day-to-day use on everyday, not-too-tough dirt.

Hot water with a squirt of mild dishwashing liquid is a good for wiping off or washing surfaces.

Mix a solution of 1 part vinegar to 1 part water in a spray bottle and use as a general-purpose cleaner for worktops, tiles, and sinks.

Make a mild abrasive cleaner by adding a few drops of water to baking soda (sodium bicarbonate) to form a paste.

1 tablespoon of household bleach in 1 gallon of water makes a good disinfectant for wiping down surfaces, washing trash containers, or soaking items such as brushes and combs.

4 tablespoons of baking soda (sodium bicarbonate) in 1 quart of warm water is good for wiping out refrigerators and ovens.

Well Oiled

Make the most
of the nourishing
and moisturizing
properties of oil in your
cleaning routines.

olive oil

A dab of olive oil on a duster brings a sheen to wood and picku up dirt as well. Alternatively, mix vinegar and olive oil in equal parts for a more thorough job. **PS Don't use your best extra-virgin olive oil; go for something more refined or opt for sunflower oil.**

baby oil

If your trendy stainless steel backsplash, refrigerator, or stove is looking a bit streaky, try a little baby oil on a lint-free cloth. For a more polished finish on vinyl and linoleum floors, add a capful of baby oil to the cleaning water.

danish oil and finishing oil

These thinner, easy-to-use oils are used for treating or rejuvenating wood floors, worktops, and furniture. They can be used on a more regular basis as part of the cleaning process to add extra nourishment and increase water resistance. Use sparingly on a clean, lint-free cloth and buff off any excess.

Stain Standby Kit

Swift action is always advisable to prevent spills and splashes from damaging surfaces, furnishings, and clothing. Make sure you have a few basic ingredients at hand at all times to cope with emergencies.

• **carbonated water** or club soda (soda water)
• **mild dishwashing liquid**—the eco-friendly ones are mild and noncolored
• **sponges and clean cloth rags**—a generous pile of absorbent cloths for mopping up and drying; old cut-up sheets, towels, and T-shirts are good for this
• **neutralizers**—water, milk, sugar water, salt water
• **mineral spirits**—useful for spillages of substances with nonwater solvents such as gloss paint, oils, and glues
• **biological laundry detergent**—for more stubborn stains

Stain First Aid

blot
Blot up all excess liquid using a good supply of cloth rags or sponges. Keep going until all excess moisture has been absorbed.

dilute and disperse
Dilute and disperse any stain with a fizzy liquid like carbonated water.

dab
Blot up the diluting liquid by dabbing with a clean, dry cloth.

rub
Rub the stain with cloths or sponges dipped in a mild solution of dishwashing liquid. Work inward to avoid spreading the stain. For darker stains, apply biological laundry detergent and leave for a while.

rinse

Rinse using clean rags or a sponge and clean water.

dry

Dry as much as possible by dabbing and blotting with clean, dry cloths.

treat

If necessary, treat any remaining stain with a purpose-made stain remover but remember to read the instructions carefully. Sometimes it is necessary to let the stain dry before treatment.

2 Tools of the Trade

You are more likely to be inspired to start cleaning if you have the right tools. Basic cleaning equipment is mostly inexpensive and, with all those bright colors, cheerful enough to turn a chore into pleasure.

Basic Cleaning Kit

- floor mop
- mop bucket
- broom with fine bristles
- collection of scourers
- dustpan and brush
- cotton dishcloths (minimum of 4)
- floor / heavy-duty cloths (minimum of 2)
- cotton dusters (minimum of 3)
- feather duster / synthetic fluffy duster
- long-handled brush / feather duster
- plastic bucket(s)
- plastic bowl(s)
- large pile of clean rags (old dishtowels, bath towels, T-shirts, etc.)
- rubber gloves (3 pairs—1 pair for the kitchen, 1 pair for the bathroom, 1 pair for the toilet)

10 Extra Tools

These everyday items often do the job better than any sophisticated, specially designed gadgets or gizmos.

old toothbrushes are great for scrubbing around faucets

artists' paintbrushes are perfect for cleaning fluff off keyboards and for other delicate dusting jobs

long-handled dishwashing brushes can reach parts other, bigger implements can't—and they're better than cloths or sponges if you have long nails! There are numerous uses for **nail brushes**, including scrubbing showerheads and tile grout

cotton wool is suitably absorbent for tasks such as stain and limescale removal

use **small metal scrapers** for scraping off
dried food, spots of paint, or greasy deposits

cotton-tipped swabs soaked in water or something
stronger can be poked into all sorts of places

cocktail sticks are good for forcing dirt
out of corners, ridges, and holes

wire coat hangers can be
unwound and used to probe
inaccessible places and, in an
emergency, to unblock the toilet

The Brushoff

Dirt and crumbs make a place look neglected and unclean, but a quick sweep is often all that's needed.

broom
Soft bristles are best for sweeping up fine dust and hairs and getting into corners and along baseboards.

dustpan and brush
A dustpan and brush can be used in conjunction with a broom or on their own for a quick sweep up. Most are plastic but it is possible to buy old-fashioned metal dustpans, which look great but can scratch the floor. A long-handled dustpan and brush cut out the need for a broom and for bending down.

short-handled brush
Useful for brushing off dust and debris and raising the pile on rugs and carpets (especially stairs), and for getting into, underneath, and around awkward spaces and objects. The brush that comes with the dustpan is fine but you may want an extra one that is clean enough for use on fabrics and carpets.

brush care

To prolong the life and efficiency of your brooms, brushes, and dustpans, wash them regularly in warm soapy water. Rinse well and allow to dry thoroughly before use.

If possible leave
mops outside to dry—it
will stop them from
getting smelly.

Mopping Up

Mopping is a quick, easy, and effective way to remove the dirt.

mop

Squeezy mops used to be all the rage, but they are no good for corners so the **old-fashioned mop**, recently reinvented made out of strips of cloth, is back in favor. The new versions are light and easy to use but it is still possible to get the old string mops, which soak up a satisfying amount of water and allow you to apply a bit more force, especially if you have large areas to clean. Replace mopheads when they become thin and straggly.

bucket

Plastic buckets with a place to squeeze the mop are essential. If you want to play at being a janitor, you can opt for the galvanized bucket and stringy mop, but beware—the bucket is heavy and clattery and can scratch sensitive floors. Look for the **double bucket** with one side for soapy water and the other for clean water for rinsing.

Tools of the Trade

41

The Importance of a Good Cloth

You will make a better job of cleaning if you have a good cloth. Those throw-away cloths somehow just don't do the business, they leave too much dampness behind and are not man enough for tough jobs. What's more, they are expensive and not very eco-friendly. Invest in proper, grownup cloths. Natural fibers are best; they are more absorbent and can be wrung out more thoroughly. Cotton and linen have a texture that gives a bit of friction, essential for a good rub down.

Be thrifty and eco-minded and recycle old bath towels, dishtowels, sheets, pillowcases, and T-shirts, giving them a new purposeful life as dusters, polishers, dishcloths, floor cloths, window cleaners, and general wipers down and moppers up.

If you don't have enough rags, look on market stalls where you can buy towels and dishcloths at very low prices.

clean cloths

Cloth hygiene is very important as dirty and wet cloths are the perfect breeding ground for bacteria. Kill the bacteria by **soaking** cloths **regularly** in a solution of bleach. Rinse out cloths after use in cold water—bugs absolutely love warm rags, but won't hang around to breed in cold conditions.

44

Division of Labor

It may seem obvious but don't forget to segregate your cleaning cloths and sponges, after all you wouldn't wash your face in the sink using a dishcloth any more than you would clean the toilet with a washcloth.

kitchen
- **dishwashing**—sponges, brushes, and dishcloths
- **sinks and worktops**—a cloth or sponge-scourer
- **floor**—even if you normally mop the floor, keep a floor cloth handy for spills and splashes
- **dishtowels**—strictly for dishes, pots, and pans
- **hand towel**—keep a separate towel for drying your hands

bathroom
- **bathtub, shower, and basin**—sponge-scourers, brushes, and cloths
- **toilet**—a cloth for washing and wiping down the seat and the outside of the toilet, and a toilet-brush for the inside

The Score on Scourers

Careless scrubbing can cause damage, so choose your scourer with care.

- **knitted plastic**—gentle yet efficient especially when used with a cream cleanser
- **knitted steel**—only to be used on tough dirt on tough objects
- **soap-impregnated steel wool**—a little messy and can scratch, but very good for removing burned-on food from ovenware and pans
- **flat nylon**—normally green and very good for all kinds of uses from tough dishwashing jobs to washing paintwork
- **sponge / scourer**—very useful and versatile, with a soft side and a tough side. Uses include dishwashing, cleaning bathtubs, and preparing surfaces for painting. The standard scourer is quite abrasive but there is also a gentler version for nonstick pans that doesn't scratch.

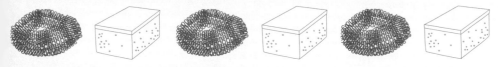

Prevent soap-filled
pan-scourers from rusting by
wrapping them in a plastic
bag and storing them in
the freezer.

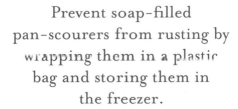

The Art of Dusting

The battle against dust can never be won because it is in the air at all times, but that is no excuse to give up. The knowledge that household dust consists mostly of flakes of dead skin, molds, insect body parts and egg cases, hairs, and flakes of cat saliva can turn even the most resolute slob into a devoted duster. Take as much pride in your dusting-cloths drawer as your underwear drawer: keep it well stocked and frequently laundered.

dust duty

• Arm yourself with clean cotton dusters and a feather duster for the less accessible areas or delicate objects.

• Start at the top and work down so that dislodged dust and dirt fall down onto undusted areas.

• Use the duster lightly since dust contains particles that can scratch and damage surfaces if you rub too hard.

• Shake out dusters frequently, otherwise you are just moving the dust around rather than getting rid of it.

• To prevent dust from flying around and settling back on the things you've just dusted, slightly dampen the duster with water.

• Have a slightly damp cloth handy for removing surface dirt and marks, such as rings from cups and glasses.

• Use a vacuum cleaner or hand-held dustbuster for corners and upholstery.

• Finish the dusting program with a thorough vacuuming.

Damp Dusting

A damp duster will pick up more dust than a dry one, as well as prevent it from flying around. However, it shouldn't be too damp. Using a spray bottle filled with water (add a few drops of lemon oil or lavender for a nice smell and more effective cleaning) will achieve the right level of dampness.

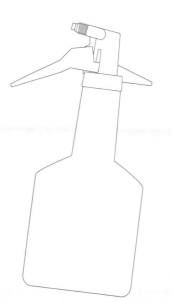

Feather Pleasure

• If dusting doesn't tickle your fancy, try a feather
duster. More fun than a boring cloth, it allows you
to dust around things without moving them.

• Perfect for dusting high shelves, it may also inspire
you to dust ledges, light fixtures, lampshades,
pictures, and precious ornaments, and even flick
the dust off the tops of books. A long-handled
feather duster allows you to get to cobwebs on the
ceiling and into all kinds of awkward spaces.

• Splash out on a good-quality feather duster
because the poor-quality ones can scratch and leave
feathery bits in their wake.

• The synthetic, fluffy dusters are also good, but
they don't get into the places feathers can reach,
are generally heavier and therefore less sensitive to
nooks and crannies, and, if you're not careful,
more prone to knocking things over.

• Shake out feather and synthetic dusters frequently
as you dust.

• Wash synthetic dusters in soapy water and rinse
well but do not use a water softener because this
reduces static, which is what picks up the dust.

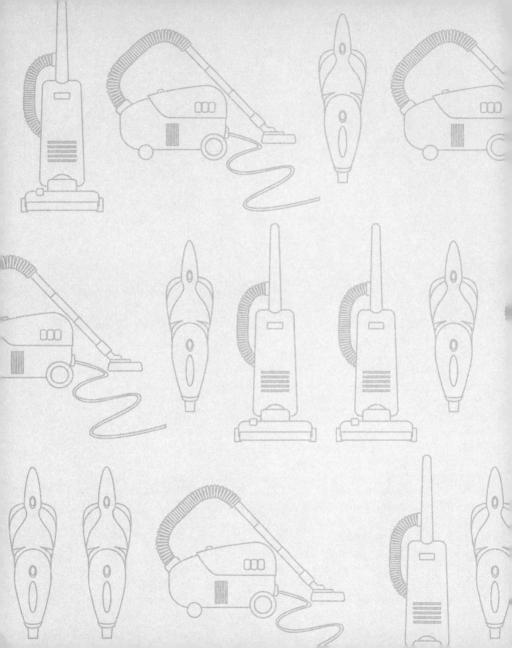

3 Clean Machines

You will make a more thorough job of cleaning with a little help from your friends the vacuum cleaner and its little helper the dustbuster.

Vacuum Cleaners

Essential for sucking dirt and dust out of your carpet, vacuum cleaners are also great for cleaning bare floors, upholstery, beds, and drapes, and for general dusting. When choosing your machine, you need to consider:

style

Choose a model that can be stored in an accessible space—you will be more likely to use it if you can get at it easily. Cylinder types are the most popular and versatile. An upright model may be easier on acres of carpet but isn't easy to carry upstairs. If you opt for this type, make sure it has a hose and long-handled attachment for stairs, corners, and edges.

attachments

The attachments are very important, so look before you buy. Ideally they will include a narrow nozzle, dusting brush, upholstery nozzle, general-purpose brush attachment, and a floor brush with bristles that won't scratch those fashionably bare floors.

power

Believe it or not, vacuum cleaners can be too powerful. Some of the super models will suck the fibers right out of your expensive carpet and the feathers out of your pillows—you have been warned! Traditional vacuum cleaners lose suction power as the bag or chamber fills up, unlike the cyclone vacuum cleaners, which work by centrifugal force and do not lose suction. Variable suction settings is a useful feature, especially for more delicate items such as drapes.

dust disposal

With a bagless vacuum cleaner dust is collected in the body of the machine and is easy to empty (and the see-through dirt chamber provides an entertaining, if sobering, view of what has been lurking in your home). Replaceable bags are also easy to dispose of but can be expensive, and wasteful, although you can reuse the bag.

10 Uses for a Vacuum Cleaner

carpets and rugs

beds

curtains and drapes

venetian blinds

bare floors

upholstery

general dusting

high cobwebs

tops of door and
window frames
and other high
surfaces

home-decorating
preparation and
cleaning up

Dustbusters

Dustbusters are small hand-held,
wirefree, battery-run vacuum cleaners that
are charged up by plugging into
a normal electric socket.

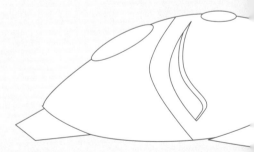

10 things dustbusters are useful for:

• quick tidy-ups for unexpected visitors
• dealing with accidental spills, such as the contents of a carelessly opened cereal packet
• getting into awkward corners, and under and behind things
• persuading teenagers to do their share
• picking up crumbs from inside cupboards
• picking up the dust from small home-immprovement jobs such as drilling holes
• cleaning out bags, baskets, and suitcases
• getting rid of hairs and other dirt from pets' beds
• removing hairs and fluff from clothing
• cleaning inside cars

4 Beasts, Bugs, and Bacteria

We are surrounded by millions of microbes. Most are harmless, some can make us sick, and a few, such as salmonella bacteria, can make us very ill. Infections are mostly associated with food hygiene so it's worth developing good habits in the kitchen. But don't go overboard. Exposure to bacteria and viruses helps build up immunity, so a sterile environment in your own home would make you vulnerable to otherwise mild bugs you may pick up outside.

Allergy Alert

Allergies are an adverse reaction to allergens. While some reactions can be dangerous, others are mild. An adverse reaction may be a "sensitivity" rather than a full-blown allergy. A number of allergens are present in air and household dust, including VOCs (volatile organic compounds) that are vapors released from chemicals found in household cleaners, air fresheners, paints, and stain removers.

action
• Keep the dust down with regular
dusting and vacuuming
• Launder bed linen, towels, other
household textiles, and clothes frequently
• Keep dust-gathering clutter to
a minimum
• Avoid "magic" cleaning products
that contain harsh chemicals
• Maintain good ventilation

common reactions
headaches
skin rashes
breathing problems, including asthma
nausea
dizziness
sore throat
itchy nose

common allergens
fungal spores
faeces, egg cases, and dead body parts of insects
hairs and faeces of rodents
chemicals used in cleaning products, air-fresheners,
   and paints

common sources
damp
mold
dust mites (see page 72)
cockroaches
cats, dogs, and birds

Beasts, Bugs, and Bacteria

Unwelcome Visitors

We share our homes with a vast number of living creatures. While most are harmless, some are a potential health threat. Grimy surfaces, open packets of food, crumbs, last night's leftovers, and unwashed dishes provide a running buffet for many of these hungry creatures.

Flies bring in and spread bacteria. They not only eat your food but lay eggs on it, which soon hatch out into maggots that grow into more flies.

Cockroaches can carry dangerous diseases such as dysentery, gastroenteritis, and typhoid. As well as food, they also enjoy hair, leather, wallpaper, and faeces.

Fleas prefer pets, but they sometimes bite humans. Their eggs—often laid in carpets—can lay dormant for years until a suitable tasty dog or cat comes along.

Moths lay their eggs on your best clothes, linens, and carpets, which become food for the hatched maggots.

Mosquitos spread malaria, but not all of them do. However, the bites itch like mad.

Mice spread germs and droppings, and the fact that they pee as they run along is enough to put anyone off.

Rats carry Weils disease—a nasty and potentially fatal illness caught by contact with their urine. No one in their right mind wants rats in their home.

Pest Deterrents

There are plenty of effective insecticides and poisons on the market, but many are toxic and therefore dangerous, especially if you have pets and young children. They can also provoke allergic reactions. If you have a real "infestation" of insects or vermin, you are advised to call in the professionals. Otherwise, try these more friendly deterrents.

Insects don't like strong smells so burning eucalyptus, lavender, citronella, wintergreen, or peppermint oil on an oil burner will keep them away. **Mosquitos** in particular dislike citronella. **Moths** will leave your linens alone if you store them with cotton-wool balls dipped in lavender, eucalyptus, or rosemary oil.

Scented plants also help. Try basil and verbena for **flies**, while mint will deter **ants**.

If the **ants** persist, try sprinkling red pepper or chili powder at their point of entry.

Trapping is okay for one or two troublesome **mice** (bait traps with dried fruit, not cheese). If you can't face dead bodies, use a humane trap and release the miscreant back into the wild, preferably somewhere far away. If you are brave, you can try to trap a **rat** (they love Brazil nuts), but rats rarely live alone so it is best to contact a specialty company who will send in the rat-catcher.

Catching Cockroaches

You can make your own pesticide-free trap using a **jar** with a **slice of white bread** inside. A **piece of wood**, such as a ruler, will help them get into the jar and a coating of **petroleum jelly** on the inside of the jar mouth will make the cockroaches fall in and also stop them from escaping. They can be killed with hot soapy water or by placing them in the freezer overnight. Alternatively, adding borax to the bait will kill them, but don't use this if there are children or pets in the house.

Dust Mites— The Awful Truth

Too small to be seen with the naked eye, these tiny aracnids thrive in warm, moist places and feast on flakes of dead skin. Unsurprisingly their ideal homes include mattresses, pillows, and bedding, but they are happy to take up residence in carpets, pillows, upholstered furniture, and soft toys. They don't spread disease but the dust from their dead bodies and egg cases are the allergens that can provoke allergies in humans, especially asthmatics.

5 ways to fight the mite

1 Wash bed linen at a minimum of 130°F.
2 Avoid padded headboards. Opt for a wood or metal-framed bed with open slats.
3 Clutter attracts dust, so keep it under control.
4 Mites can be killed by freezing, so put feather and down comforters, pillows, and soft toys in a chest freezer for at least six hours every six months or so—or more if they are a big problem. This kills the mites, but not the allergens, which will have to be removed by washing.
5 Avoid wall-to-wall carpets and drapes and opt instead for bare floors, washable rugs, and window shades or blinds.

Now Wash Your Hands... Properly!

Amazingly, people are getting very lazy about washing their hands. Some don't bother, while others make do with a quick, ineffective rinse and a wipe on a microbe-laden towel. Make sure you wash your hands properly before and after handling food. You know it makes sense.

1 Wet your hands.
2 Soap thoroughly and rub your hands together, making sure you get in between the fingers—and don't forget the backs of your hands and wrists.
3 Scrub your nails if you have been handling raw meat, tackling a very dirty job, or digging the garden.
4 Rinse the bar of soap or the liquid soap container (you don't want to leave it covered in bacteria).
5 Rinse your hands thoroughly under clean, running water.
6 Dry thoroughly on a clean towel rubbing briskly to remove any remaining microbes. Wet hands spread germs much more effectively than dry.

Don't forget to change hand
towels frequently as they
often harbor bugs and
bacteria passed from less
well-washed hands and less
scrupulous users.

Food Watch

If you've ever had food poisoning, you are unlikely to want to repeat the experience. As most cases are caused by infections picked up in the home, it is worth taking a few precautions in food areas even if the rest of your home is less than pristine.

keep clean

Make sure there is no food left around in any form, including crumbs and smears. Wash your hands before and after handling food and in between different foodstuffs, such as meat or fish.

keep dry

Bugs dislike dry surfaces and atmospheres so keep everywhere well ventilated and keep foodstuffs in airtight containers. Don't keep food in packets if your cupboards are damp.

keep cool

Run refrigerators and freezers at the correct temperature—a maximum of 37°F for a refrigerator and 0°F for a freezer—and, if possible, store other foodstuffs in cool places.

keep tidy

Clutter provides more opportunities and more surfaces for dust and dirt to settle and for insects and bacteria to accumulate and breed.

food bug danger zones:

hands
sinks and bowls
dishcloths
worktops
chopping boards
garbage containers

5 Bacteria Killers

Chlorine bleach is effective on most household germs and is useful for wiping down worktops and soaking cleaning cloths and items such as hairbrushes and even children's toys. Use neat for pouring down toilets, sinks, and waste pipes, but always dilute it with water for other general uses.

· Wiping down worktops and surfaces:
3 tablespoons to 1 gallon of water
· Soaking fabrics, cleaning cloths, hairbrushes, toys, etc.: 1 tablespoon to 1 gallon of water, leave for 45 minutes, and rinse thoroughly.
· Soaking overnight: 2½ teaspoons to 1 gallon of water, rinse well; keep a solution in a spray bottle for use on worktops and chopping boards.

Vinegar is a natural, nontoxic disinfectant. Use for wiping surfaces clean and for cleaning kitchen and bathroom sinks: 1 part vinegar to 1 part water.

Tea-tree oil is a natural disinfectant and deodorizer and is also effective as a fungicide. Wipe down surfaces with a solution of 2 teaspoons of tea-tree oil and 2 cups of water, or put it in a spray bottle for use on mold and mildew.

Borax is a disinfectant, insecticide, and deodorizer. Mixed with baking soda it makes a good general-purpose germ-killing cleaner and can also be used for soaking fabrics.

Heat kills a lot of bacteria. Washing bed linen, towels, and cleaning cloths at 130°F helps keep the bugs at bay. Boiling is good for dishcloths and boiling water can be poured onto utensils and chopping boards or down waste pipes.

Solar Power

Sunshine is the best natural disinfectant and various items in your home will benefit from a sunbathing session. The sun's heat and rays kill bacteria and creatures such as dust mites. If you have a garden, patio, or balcony, put them outside; if you haven't, then don't be afraid to hang things out of the window, European-style. If possible, dry your laundry outdoors.

10 items to benefit from a day in the sun

- feather and down comforters and bed pillows
- bedspreads, blankets, and throws
- mattresses—futons will love it
- children's toys—especially soft ones
- throw pillows—the sun fluffs up the feathers
- rugs, dhurries, and kilims
- anything with pet and urine stains
- fabric stains—they will fade in the sun
- clothes that are dry-cleaned rather than washed
- shoes especially sneakers; take the laces out and
open them up to the sunshine

Spore Wars

Edible fungi are delicious, but the kind of fungi that inhabit your refrigerator or grow on your walls, shower curtains, and in between your toes are not so appetizing. There are millions of spores, yeasts, molds, and mildew flying around your home looking for somewhere to live and breed. They are common components of house dust and can cause allergies and infections. They love damp, moist conditions so are most happy in **steamy bathrooms** and **unventilated spaces** where they make themselves visible in the form of **black spots** and splodges, which can grow at an alarming rate.

Given the chance, they **rot wood** and walls and can carry **infections**, such as ringworm and athlete's foot. At the extreme end, they cause Legionnaires disease, which is a killer. Fungal spores also invade humidifiers, dehumidifiers, and vaporizers, and set up home in tile grout, sealants, refrigerator drip trays, and food. The best defence against these invaders is to avoid damp conditions through **good ventilation** and **good housekeeping**.

Coming Up For Air

Nowadays we tend to work and live in heated, air-conditioned, double-glazed, sealed microclimates that create warm, moist, stuffy environments much enjoyed by bugs and bacteria. Poor ventilation can cause headaches, sore throats, allergies, and unpleasant smells. One of the easiest ways to remedy this situation is to open a window.

5 reasons to throw open a window

1 **Let** out stale air, steam, exhaled breath, perspiration, and cooking smells.

2 **Give** some of those flakes of skin, insect body parts, and other unwholesome ingredients of dust the chance to escape.

3 **Keep** air circulating—essential for good health and preventing the buildup of moisture.

4 **Avoid** a buildup of VOCs (volatile organic compounds) given off by common household products, paint, adhesives, and substances such as fire-retardants present in many carpets and fabrics.

5 **Replenish** the air and reduce the effects of negative ions caused by static from computers, etc.

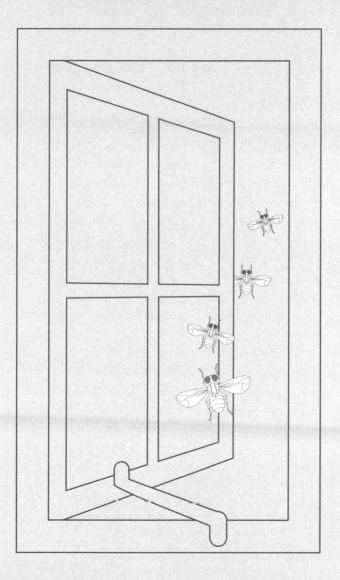

Olfactory Outlets

WARNING!

Bad smells are caused by a variety of things including damp, mildew, rotten food, dirt, and fetid footwear. Although some are short-term and unavoidable, many are the result of poor hygiene and ventilation. However, we have become oversensitive when it comes to smells; this paranoia is fed by the adverts for air "fresheners" that keep our homes free from odors, which may suggest we are anything but clean-living, sweet-smelling, bacteria-free citizens.

No one would deny the advantage of a quick burst of air freshener in the bathroom but "deodorizing" every room is not only overdoing it but dangerous. It has recently been reported that these products might cause respiratory problems, especially in babies, young children, and those with asthma. Air fresheners work either by masking the smell with a strong, synthetic odor or by desensitizing our sense of smell by coating the nasal passages with a film or blocking the olfactory nerve. Desensitization could be dangerous because it could render us unable to smell bad food or something burning.

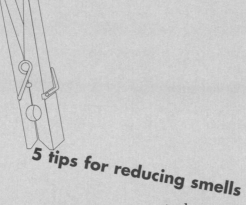

5 tips for reducing smells

1 open a window
2 install an extractor fan
3 when cooking fish, place a small bowl of
white vinegar next to the stove
4 a lighted candle in the kitchen during
cooking also reduces smells
5 vanilla extract on a cotton-wool ball in
the bathroom is an effective deodorizer

Smell As Sweet

It is easy to scent your home naturally, which is not only safer and nicer, but much less expensive, too.

essential oils

A few drops of your favorite essential oil in a small amount of water in the top of an oil burner will scent a room subtly and safely. Alternatively, try a dab of fragrant oil on a light bulb.

plants and flowers

Scented plants and cut flowers are the best of natural smells, but be careful because some of the more highly scented can be overwhelming in a small room and can cause an allergic reaction. Place scented plants near windows and doors.

herbs and spices

• Sprinkle cinnamon, nutmeg, and cloves in a small pan of water and simmer.
• Put lavender or herbs in the bag or cylinder of your vacuum cleaner.
• Put a handful of crushed, dried herbs such as rosemary or lavender in a jar with 2 tablespoons baking soda, shake well, and sprinkle on carpets and rugs. Leave for an hour before vacuuming up.

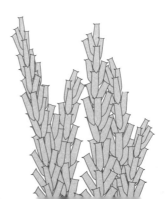

Beasts, Bugs, and Bacteria

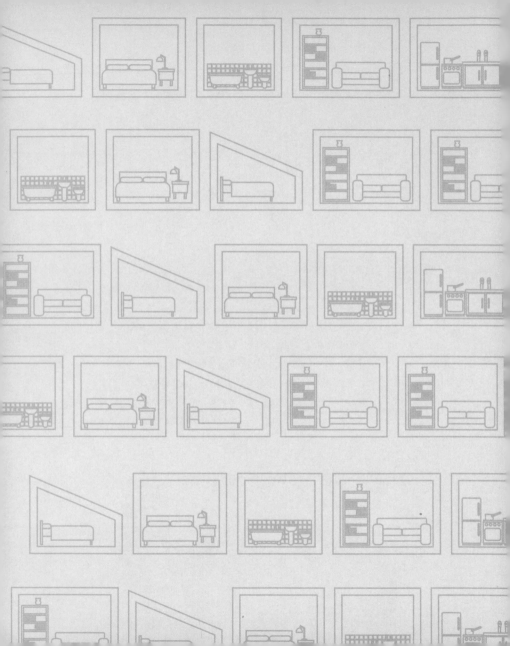

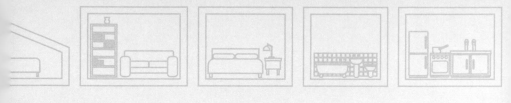

5 Order of Service

For many of us, the words "routine" and "order" are a turnoff, but when it comes to cleaning a little of both can save time and effort and bring harmony to the home.

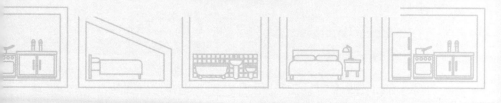

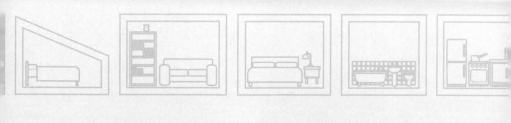

Living Areas

regular routine

Regular cleaning keeps your home looking good and makes you feel better.

daily freshening up

• open windows
• clear away dirty dishes, last night's pizza, and any clothes (especially sneakers and socks)
• plump up throw pillows and armchair and couch cushions
• remove any dirt or spills on the floor with a dustbuster or damp cloth

weekly cleaning

• open windows
• dust all surfaces
• vacuum all floors, then mop bare floors
• remove old newspapers and magazines

monthly thorough-cleaning

• shake and plump up pillows and cushions first—
if you do it later, you will add dust to already
dusted areas
• dust all surfaces plus the individual objects on
them—there is no need to clear bookshelves, but
dust the shelves and the tops of the books
• don't forget ledges, the tops of pictures, and the
legs of chairs, tables, and other furniture
• dust slatted window shades using a duster, special
gadget, or vacuum cleaner attachment
• take seat cushions off armchairs and couches,
and use the appropriate attachments to vacuum
upholstery, heavy drapes, and roller shades
• vacuum floors using attachments for edges,
corners, tops of baseboards, and underneath
furniture; if you are very houseproud, you will
move couches and chairs in order to clean the
floor underneath
• mop bare floors using appropriate methods
(see pages 200–205)

Bedroom Routines

daily

- open windows—even ten minutes is helpful
- pull the covers back to allow the bed to air
- plump up the pillows
- put dirty clothes in the laundry basket
- put clothing to be worn again on a chair to allow it to air
- remove any mugs, glasses, plates, or old food

weekly (or every other week, depending on your standards)

- remove pillowcases, down comforter cover, and bottom sheet
- turn the mattress over (especially if it is a futon)
- sort out clothes and put dirty clothes and bed linen in the laundry basket
- return clothes, shoes, and accessories to their rightful places
- dust all surfaces, starting at the highest points and working down

- use a damp cloth to wipe up stains such as spilled make-up
- empty wastepaper baskets
- remake the bed with clean bed linen
- vacuum the floor and mop any bare floors

monthly
- vacuum under the bed
- vacuum the mattress (at least every six months)

Bedtime Stories

- On average, we spend approximately a third of our lives in bed.
- During sleep our body loses around a cup of water from perspiration which ends up in our sheets, blankets, and the mattress.
- Because we spend so long in bed, the quality of air in the bedroom is more important than in any other room.
- Most asthma attacks happen at night, probably triggered by several hours of exposure to dust, poor ventilation, and airborne microbes and allergens.
- The less cluttered and messy your bedroom, the better you sleep.
- Every time you turn over you shed hundreds of flakes of dead skin—heaven for dust mites.
- While sleeping even the cleanest, most perfumed people exude skin oils and body smells, and breathe out moisture, breath smells, and microorganisms into the air, pillow, and bedding. Two in a bed doubles the amounts.

Kitchen Drill

✔ daily

- put away all foodstuffs, and if they are kept on open shelves, make sure they are in airtight, bacteria-proof containers
- wash dishes
- wipe clean all work surfaces and remove spills and splodges

✔ weekly

- clean all work surfaces and underneath appliances, such as mixers, toasters, and any other items stored on worktops
- clean the stovetop thoroughly
- throw out old and bad food—make sure nothing nasty is lurking at the back of the refrigerator
- wipe down the outside of the refrigerator
- clean the floor
- empty the trash containers and wash out

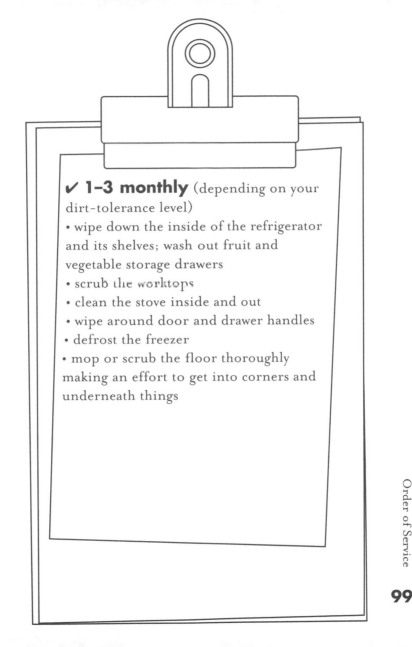

✔ 1–3 monthly (depending on your dirt-tolerance level)
• wipe down the inside of the refrigerator and its shelves; wash out fruit and vegetable storage drawers
• scrub the worktops
• clean the stove inside and out
• wipe around door and drawer handles
• defrost the freezer
• mop or scrub the floor thoroughly making an effort to get into corners and underneath things

Bathroom Routine

daily

• hang up all towels and bathmats to allow the air to circulate and dry them
• mop up any obvious puddles
• rinse any scum from the basin and bathtub—use a sponge, cloth, or quick blast of spray cleaner
• leave the shower curtain in a closed position to dry and prevent the growth of smelly mold

weekly (no excuses—if you don't do this weekly, you are a slob)

• launder all used towels and bathmats
• clear surfaces to prepare them for cleaning
• empty the wastepaper basket
• clean the toilet
• clean the bathtub, shower, and basin
• wipe down all surfaces, including tiles and mirrors (a spray cleaner is quick and easy)
• vacuum the floor first to remove dust, then mop or, as bathroom floors are usually relatively small, get on your hands and knees to give it a good scrub
• put out fresh towels and bathmats

When running a bath, put the cold water in first because this reduces the steam produced

6 Clean and Tidy

With copious quantities of dirt and dust swirling around the atmosphere waiting to settle on any available surface, it makes sense to provide the minimum opportunity for it to do so. Storing things away is the key.

Kitchen Tidy

Keep surfaces
as clear as
possible to
allow for easy,
and thorough,
cleaning.

5 ways to keep things out of the way

1 Cupboards and drawers protect objects from dust and grease.

2 Open shelves look nice, provide an opportunity for display, and keep things off work surfaces and tabletops.

3 Even if you are not a keen cook, a "batterie de cuisine" of pots, pans, and utensils hanging in your kitchen will look impressive whether hung on a purpose-made rack or on butchers' hooks on a simple pole.

4 Store unruly foodstuffs in airtight containers (but keep the labels for reference, i.e., instructions, sell-by dates). Tuck them away in a cupboard or admire them on open shelves.

5 A trash container fixed to the inside of a cupboard door or in a purpose-built unit leaves the floor clear and easier to clean.

Clean and Tidy

Tidy Your Bedroom

Your mother wasn't just nagging when she told you to tidy your bedroom. Leaving clothes, tissues, mugs, and plates lying around is bad for the clothes, bad for hygiene, and bad for your image... so start tidying up.

Keeping your best clothes under wraps is a good idea, but always use breathable plastic or fabric covers.

Air circulation in a closet will deter moths, dust mites, and mildew and help prevent that fusty, thrift-store smell from developing. If your closet is airless, open the door occasionally.

Now that you know all about perspiration, shedding skin, and those dust mites, you may want to think twice before putting today's sweater (slightly damp and with a fresh supply of skin scales) back in the drawer with the clean stuff. Allow clothes to air by hanging them up on a hook or placing them over the back of a chair or loosely folded on the seat.

A free-standing hanging rail, whether as an inexpensive alternative to a closet or a solution for overspill, is a good idea, but keep clothes dust-free by covering with a sheet or an attractive, lightweight printed fabric.

It is sensible to utilize space under the bed for extra storage, but don't just shove everything out of sight. Keep things in boxes, baskets, or purpose-made under-bed storage containers, some of which have castors for ease of access to the contents and for cleaning.

You know it makes
sense to lock away all
drugs to prevent them
from getting into
the wrong hands—
and mouths.

Bathroom Storage

cabinet secrets

Keeping a bathroom clean requires a lot of effort, but it is easier if you avoid cluttering up shelves, windowsills, and surfaces with all those lotions and potions essential for keeping you clean and beautiful. Clusters of bottles, boxes, sprays, plastic containers, and dispensers are rarely attractive—and some products are best kept private—so keep them out of sight in a good looking cabinet. This will not only make your bathroom look better, but will be easier to keep clean.

practical display

As any interiors magazine will tell you, pretty bottles, piles of towels, washcloths, sponges, and soaps transform your bathroom into something special. However, display can easily turn into clutter that makes cleaning a difficult and tedious exercise. Displaying such things in attractive bowls, baskets, and other containers will make cleaning easier. But don't forget to clean those out occasionally as well!

Clean and Tidy

Clean Living

It is easier to keep the living room clean (and tidy) if you:

keep stuff to a minimum

You don't have to be a minimalist but control the spread of pillows, bric-a-brac, unnecessary pieces of furniture, and other clutter.

keep stuff off the floor

If you provide a shelf, surface, or storage cabinet for anything and everything from magazines to coffee cups, you are less likely to suffer from shrinking floorspace.

think big

Overdesigned storage containers are often shunned by those not devoted to interior design, but even reluctant slobs might be tempted to put newspapers, CDs, or toys into large, attractive baskets and boxes. These also make a quick tidy-up a lot easier.

litter bug

Provide a wastepaper basket—it might come in handy.

keep behind closed doors

Open shelves may be one of the great storage successes of recent times but can descend into messy chaos in the wrong hands. Cupboards rather than open shelves create an aura of calm even if chaos lurks behind the door. If you want to keep control but still have things on display, go for glass-fronted cabinets.

File Away

If you don't enjoy cleaning at the best of times, it's even more daunting when your home appears to have been invaded by the paper monster who has deposited piles of paperwork, junk mail, newspapers, and magazines on every available surface. Dealing with paper piles need not be too painful if you set up a simple, uncomplicated filing system. Get rid of the piles and the dust, and detritus will have fewer places to hide.

Stage 1 **Save** or **Dump** (every week or every other week)

Stage 2 Recyle all the **Dump** and then divide the **Save** into **Do Now** and **Do Later** (every week or every other week)

Stage 3 File all the **Do Later** (whenever you have the time or the inclination)

basic equipment

To make filing easy and encourage others to join in, equip yourself with storage containers that look nice on their own, are big enough, and preferably don't have a lid—the removal of which might be too much for some to cope with. Suggestions are:

- **baskets**—an attractive asset to any home and available in a wide variety of shapes and sizes.
- **cardboard magazine holders**—perfect for magazines but also good for archiving any paperwork. Why not have several of these holders and skip straight to Stage 3?
- **bulldog clips**—great for keeping papers under control and for filing by subject. Look for big fat clips in bright colors. Can be hung on hooks.

What's the Hook?

Putting things away takes time and commitment, and for many it is something they are totally disinclined to do. If opening drawers and cabinets is a daunting prospect, try a hook, probably the simplest form of storage. To encourage children (and childish adults), invest in novelty hooks; there are loads available decorated with pictures or made in the shape of animals.

get hooked
- **hallway**—coats, bags, baskets, shoes, keys, umbrellas, sports equipment
- **kitchen**—dishcloths, rubber gloves, dishtowels, towels, aprons
- **bathroom**—towels, washcloths, bathmats, laundry bags, make-up bags
- **bedroom**—clothes, accessories, laundry bags, jewelry, scarves
- **backs of doors**—clothes, laundry bags, shoe bags
- **anywhere**—bulldog-clipped bills, correspondence, lists, recipes, and anything else you need easy access to

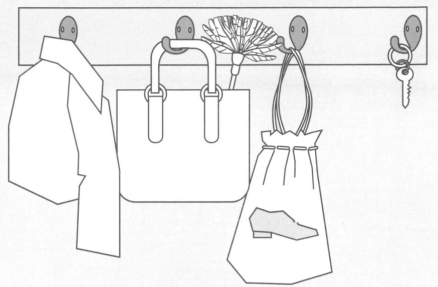

Don't waste the storage opportunities of hung-up bags and baskets, which can be filled with everything from shoes, gloves, and scarves to dusters and general junk.

7 Water Features

Even if you neglect the rest of your home, wherever water is involved deserves special attention since these are the places where hygiene is likely to be an issue. Be aware that stains can also be a stain on your character and that dirty sinks, bathtubs, showers, and toilets can provoke a number of reactions from mild disgust to outright condemnation.

Limescale

what is it?

Limescale is formed from the deposits in "hard" water, which is high in dissolved minerals, mostly calcium and magnesium.

what does it do?

Although it is not a health risk, it causes a hard, beige-brown buildup on and around faucets, shower fixtures, sinks, and inside kettles. Not only is it unsightly, it affects performance. It clogs up the little holes in showerheads reducing power, and a buildup in electric kettles, washing and dishwashing machines, and hot-water heating systems affects efficiency and energy use. If you have a big problem, you might want to install a water-softening system, or use water-softening agents in washing machines and dishwashers.

Although it is an effective limescale remover, vinegar is an acid that, if used too strong and for too long, will eat into the surface of an enameled bathtub, dulling its appearance and making it less dirt-resistant.

limescale removal

As limescale consists mostly of calcium, which is an alkali, it needs an acid to dissolve it. There are several efficient, descaling products on the market but vinegar is a simpler and cheaper alternative. A wipe or scrub with a cloth dipped in neat vinegar will remove light deposits but a bigger buildup requires more effort.

Remove showerheads and soak in a solution of 1 part water to 1 part vinegar. Scrub off any remaining deposits using a nail- or toothbrush and, if necessary, use a needle or pin to poke it out of the holes.

To remove limescale from faucets, fill a plastic bag with cotton wool soaked in a generous amount of vinegar. Place the bag over the faucet making sure the vinegary cotton wool is touching the affected parts, and put a rubber band around the neck of the bag to prevent the vinegar from seeping out.

Keep on top of the limescale by spraying sinks, showers, and bathtubs regularly with a weak vinegar solution; leave for a few minutes before rinsing off.

Water Features

Dirty Scum

what is it?

Soaps and detergents combine with the mineral salts in water to form the scum that gets left behind on sinks, bathtubs, shower trays, and tiles. It builds up over time to form a dull, grayish film. Along with the scum there is bound to be a certain amount of dirt and grease from the washing of bodies and dishes, all of which is attractive to bacteria, mold, and mildew and unattractive to fellow washers and bathers.

preventative measures

As with all dirt, a quick spray with a good old vinegar and water solution or proprietary spray cleaner after bathing or showering will keep the scum away.

If you can't be bothered to spritz after each bath or shower, use a cream or general-purpose cleanser at least once a week. Rinse well and wipe off with a dry cloth or towel.

big scum

If no one has done either of the above or you have just moved into a new property previously inhabited by scummy people, you have to exert more effort. This mostly means using a nonscratch scourer and extra cleaning material. A mildly abrasive cream cleanser is good, although a spray cleanser is easier to apply—buy one specially formulated for getting rid of soap scum. Because soap scum is mostly alkali and body dirt is mostly acidic you need a two-pronged attack using both vinegar and baking soda or their commercial equivalents.

Using a bath foam reduces the amount of scum left behind.

Mildew

what is it?

When some of those millions of fungal spores flying around us find a nice damp, warm place to live they breed and form ever-expanding unsightly, black growths that give off a fusty, musty smell. Danger zones are tiles—especially the grouting and sealants around sinks, bathtubs, and showers.

prevention

Keep the atmosphere as dry as possible with good ventilation and frequent wiping down of wet surfaces. If you have a severe moisture problem, install a fan.

cure

Specialty mildew treatments are available that are efficient and easy to use, but good results can be achieved with homemade alternatives.

For **general staining**, spray with a bleach solution (²⁄₃ cup household bleach in 3 pints of water), leave for half an hour, scrub, and rinse.

For **tougher, blacker stains**, make a paste with borax and lemon juice or vinegar, leave on for half an hour, and scrub off.

To remove mildew from **tile grout**, mix 2 parts baking soda, 1 part borax, and enough hot water to make a thick paste, apply to grout, and scrub with a soft brush, then rinse well.

To remove mold from **sealant** around the bathtub, sinks, and shower trays, wipe with neat vinegar then wipe with a paste of baking soda.

In Sink

A dirty sink is not only a health hazard, it says something about its owner.

cleaning

Use a good squirt of multipurpose liquid or cream cleanser or, if you are into alternatives, a paste of baking soda and water. A sponge scourer (the softer, nonscratch variety) is best because it can be flipped over to scrub heavier dirt.

stains

Water spots and rust marks can usually be removed with a little extra cleanser and a little more effort, but if they refuse to budge, try giving them a good rub with a soft cloth dipped in neat vinegar.

exceptions and observations

Stainless steel sinks are very robust, hygienic, and easy to clean. But don't expect new sinks to retain that brilliant shine; accept that they will develop a more muted, matte glow.

Enameled sinks scratch easily and also chip, so be careful with those heavy pans. Avoid harsh abrasives and scourers and acid-based cleaning products.

Porcelain sinks are unforgiving if you drop anything, so be careful. They develop a crazed surface over time, which can lead to staining. To freshen them up and remove stains, fill with a water and bleach solution and leave for half an hour.

Acrylic sinks should be treated more gently. Don't use harsh abrasives or scourers. Follow any manufacturer's instructions.

Composite materials can be cleaned using mild cream cleanser and a soft scourer. For stains, follow the manufacturer's instructions, which may advise the use of a fine abrasive paper.

Kitchen Sink Drama

Allowing tea leaves, coffee grounds, and small pieces of food to go down the drain is asking for trouble. Blockages are not pleasant and bad ones can require drastic action. Stop stuff going down the waste pipe by covering the drain hole with a sink strainer, and get into the habit of pouring boiling water down the waste pipe occasionally to melt grease.

If the waste pipe does get blocked, there are various forms of action:

Try an old-fashioned sink plunger. Make sure you have an airtight seal around the drain hole—and if you have a double sink, make sure the other hole is plugged. Press up and down vigorously and see what happens.

Pour about $\frac{1}{3}$ cup baking soda down the drain followed by 1 cup of vinegar poured very slowly. This should create a satisfying fizz that, hopefully, will clear the blockage.

If you have any of those big fizzy indigestion-relief tablets in the medicine cabinet, pop two down the drain followed by 1 cup of vinegar.

Tip ⅓ cup salt and ⅓ cup baking powder down the drain followed by a kettleful of boiling water.

Pour down 2 tablespoons washing soda (sodium carbonate) dissolved in 1 quart of hot water.

If none of the above work, try one of the many proprietary products fo unblocking sinks. They can be expensive but are usually effective and therefore worth it, but follow the instructions carefully because they contain harsh and toxic chemicals.

The Art of Washing Dishes

Equipment...

plastic dishwashing bowl (optional) *
sponge scourer,

dishwashing brush (with a nice long
handle), bottle brush, dishcloth

* If you have a double sink, it is best to wash dishes
directly in the sink, but if not, a bowl is useful as it
allows you to use the sink while you are doing the
dishes. A bowl also provides a soft surface for delicate
dishes and prevents the sink from being scratched.

Hand Dishwashing

1 **Scrape** off food scraps.

2 **Rinse** to remove excess grease (optional, but you won't have to change the dishwashing water as often).

3 **Stack** scraped and rinsed dishes, mugs, and glasses in orderly piles.

4 **Fill** a sink or bowl with hot water and a good squirt of dishwashing liquid.

5 **Wash** glasses first, followed by the least dirty items and ending with the tough stuff. Use a scourer on dried-on food and a dishwashing brush on the insides of mugs and in between the prongs of forks.

6 **Change** the water as soon as it looks murky.

7 **Rinse** to remove suds, which leave residues that should not be ingested. Running water is best, but a more eco-friendly alternative is to dunk them in the second sink or a bowl of clean, hot water.

8 **Drain** in a dish drainer making sure any mugs, cups, bowls, and pans are upside down.

9 **Dry** either by leaving to drain or with a clean dishtowel. Have a generous stack of tea towels at hand so that you don't wipe things with a wet one.

Remove stains from teapots,
tea cups, and coffee mugs by filling
with a solution of I part baking
soda to 2 parts hot water.
If possible, leave overnight
before rinsing.

Pots and Pans

Cooking is pleasurable but doing the dishes is not so much fun. The job is less of a chore if you always fill pots, pans, and ovenware with water and a squirt of dishwashing liquid as soon as you have finished using them. If you do this, most food deposits will come off easily with the help of a scourer, if necessary.

- For **burnt-on food**, fill the ovenware with hot water, add 1 tablespoon baking soda and soak.
- Remove **burned-on stains** on old heatproof glassware with a soap-filled pad.
- Never use abrasives on **nonstick pans**; use a plastic scourer and a little of dishwashing liquid.
- To prevent **untreated cast iron** from rusting, wash by hand, dry thoroughly, then brush the inside with a thin layer of vegetable oil.
- Soak **enameled pots** in hot soapy water. Never fill a hot pan with cold water; make sure the pan has cooled before washing, rinsing, and drying. Remove stubborn residues with a plastic or sponge scourer. Pans with metal or plastic handles can be washed in a dishwasher, but those with wood handles should be washed by hand.
- Clean **aluminum pans** with a solution of ½ cup vinegar to 1 quart of water (neat vinegar eats into aluminum). Boil and then simmer for 10 minutes.
- **Stainless steel pans** develop a rainbow effect after a while. The insides can be cleaned as for aluminum or use a proprietary stainless steel cleaner.

Bathtubs and Basins

A wipe with a cream cleanser or a baking soda paste gets rid of most dirt, but you may need to use more force and more cleanser on the tidemark.

- Avoid acidic cleaners on **enamel bathtubs and sinks** because they erode the surface. A **plastic scourer** is a good nonscratch cleaning implement. Use **mineral spirits** for stains.
- It is easier to clean the **bathtub** when it is **warm**, so tackle it right away after getting out.
- Keep a spray bottle of **vinegar solution** or **proprietary cleaner** handy to spritz baths and basins immediately after use, leaving for a few minutes before rinsing off.
- A **magnetic holder** keeps **soap** dry (and hygienic) and prevents soggy soap scum clogging up the basin.
- Give **faucets** a quick polish with a little **toothpaste** (not the gel type). Rub it on with your finger, rinse, and polish with a dry cloth.
- Never use scourers or abrasives on **acrylic** bathtubs, neat **dishwashing liquid** on a soft cloth is a neat idea, as is **liquid laundry detergent** for tidemarks.
- Keep cleaning materials **handy** to encourage you (and others) to use them.

Refreshing Showers

After a shower, the last thing you want (or have time) to do is clean up after yourself. It is the polite thing to do, however, especially if you share the bathroom with others, but even if you don't, it will be more pleasant to use the next time.

The après shower habit

1 Rinse the shower tray and tiles using the showerhead.

2 Spray the tiles with vinegar solution in a spray bottle or scrape any excess water and soap off the tiles using a shower squeegee (available from bathroom catalogs and stores).

3 Open out the shower curtain to allow it to dry or wipe down the glass screen with a dry towel or cloth dedicated to that purpose.

- To remove mildew from machine-washable **shower curtains**, wash in the washing machine with laundry detergent and, if possible, several old towels that will act as scourers. Use a warm wash cycle and put I cup of white vinegar in the final rinse to deter regrowth. For non-machine-washable curtains, try scrubbing with a paste of baking soda or leaving to soak overnight in a mild bleach solution.
- Clean **fiberglass shower trays** and bathtubs with a paste of baking soda and dishwashing liquid.
- In the unlikely event that you should have some, wipe down **glass shower screens** with leftover white wine.

It goes
without saying
that toilets should
be cleaned regularly.
Don't overdo the
chemicals, however, as
some of these products
are not biodegradable
and add to the problems
of breaking down sewage
and the pollution of
our environment.

Clean Around the Bend

under the rim

Take a look under the toilet rim and you may be unpleasantly surprised at the buildup of limescale and stains. Keep on top of this by using a proprietary cleaner that is thick enough to stay in place and do its job. Apply last thing at night or before going out so it has a few hours to work. Use once or twice a week depending on the amount of toilet traffic.

under the seat

Often neglected, the underside of the toilet seat harbors more bacteria than the top. Just don't forget to include it in your cleaning program.

around the base

Along with under the seat, these two areas are the danger zones and are in most need of attention.

around the bend

Neglect this area and the horrors it harbors soon come creeping out into the open. Avoid limescale buildup with specialist toilet cleaners, fizzy tablets, or a cupful of vinegar left overnight in the toilet from time to time.

Water Features

Plunge In

The only way to get a toilet really clean is to use elbow grease. Pull on **rubber gloves**, and with a bucket or bowl of **hot sudsy water** wash down the outside and the seat—both the top and the bottom, not forgetting the hinges. Moving on to the inside, enlist the help of a **cream cleanser**, or if you are that way inclined, **baking soda** or **borax**. Do a general scrub with a **toilet brush** and then, using an old **dishwashing brush** or **toothbrush**, scrub under the rim. Using the toilet brush to push the water around the U-bend, tackle the tidemark. This may involve the use of a **scourer** or toothbrush and/or the application of **specialty limescale remover** or a mix of **borax** and **white vinegar**. Finish with an all-over wash with a weak solution of **warm sudsy water**. Dry the outside and the seat with a clean, absorbent cloth.

Now wash
your hands.

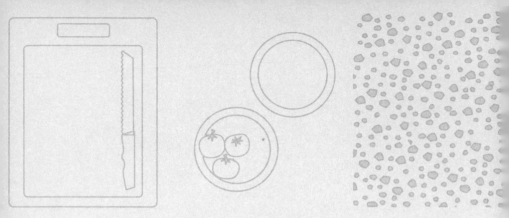
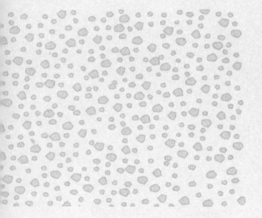
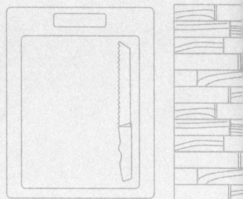

8 Surface Tension

Kitchen worktops come into contact with food and therefore there is a hygiene as well as a cleaning issue. Keeping them clear of too much debris will make them easier to clean.

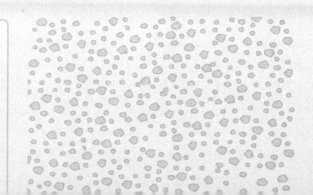
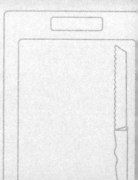

Worktop Workout

love that patina

Unless you are a perfection freak or are prepared to spend hours protecting and preserving the "as new" appearance of your worktop, you are advised to adopt a more pragmatic approach and accept that a well-used worktop will acquire a patina developed over years of use and abuse. By many, this patina is regarded as character.

For most types of worktop, a **wipe over** with a cloth wrung out in **warm sudsy water** is enough. Avoid abrasives and don't slosh too much water around as it can soak into joints and joins causing structural damage. Dried-on grime may require extra effort and an application of **baking soda** or a **cream cleaner**.

Protect surfaces by using **chopping boards**: never cut anything directly on the work surface. Not only does it spoil the appearance, it also breaks down the surface, which then attracts dirt and bacteria.

Tea and coffee spills stain so use a **tray**.

Never put hot pans or dishes straight from the oven directly onto any type of worktop because the heat causes damage; use **hot pads or trivets**.

Exceptions and Observations

wood

Make sure any wood worktop is treated with an oil that will prevent it from drying out and increase its waterproofing properties. Scrub occasionally using a nylon-mesh scourer dipped in soapy water and follow the grain. Don't allow butchers' block type surfaces to get too wet because they will fall apart—wipe with a damp cloth then dry thoroughly. Treat dry patches with a little vegetable oil.

laminate

Though hardwearing, laminated surfaces will stain and scratch. Soak hardened-on food residue by placing a not-too-wet cloth over it until things soften up. For general stains, use an all-purpose liquid cleaner applied with a cloth or soft scourer. Try lemon juice or vinegar on rust and stains.

stone

Natural stone is soluble in acid. Soft versions including **marble** and **limestone** are more porous so avoid the vinegar and acid-based cleaners and never use lemon on marble stains because it burns into the surface and the mark cannot be removed. **Granite** and **slate** are much harder and more robust but are still vulnerable to acid attack—and don't scour them too much as it makes the surface more porous. With any stone it is important to follow the manufacturer's care instructions.

Kitchen Killer

One of the most potentially dangerous items in a kitchen is the **chopping board**, which can harbor deadly bacteria as well as insect life.

The greatest danger comes from salmonella and E. coli bacteria often present in uncooked meat, especially chicken. The bacteria can live on an inadequately washed chopping board where it can be passed on through foodstuffs and on hands.

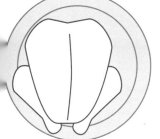

• Avoid the risk of food-poisoning by **using a separate board for meat**. Never chop or place uncooked foodstuffs on a board just used for raw meat.

• After chopping meat **wash the board** in hot, soapy water then soak for 2 minutes in a solution of 3 tablespoons bleach to I gallon water, rinse to remove bleach, and dry with a clean cloth.

• To remove smells, **rub with a lemon wedge**, baking soda, or a vinegar solution.

• Get rid of stains by **sprinkling with salt** or rubbing with lemon or a paste of baking soda.

• **Butchers' block boards** will split if soaked, so wipe them down with a bleach solution, then wipe several times with clean water and dry well.

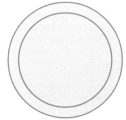

Surface Tension

9 Appliance Science

Even modest homes now have an impressive number of appliances to help us get through our busy days. It's tempting to think they look after themselves, but, in fact, they need cleaning and maintenance to keep them in working order.

Cook's Dilemma

If you survive on takeout food or ready-meals, the most important item to keep clean will be the microwave. If you cook proper meals, your stovetop, oven, and kitchen will get dirty from all the steam, grease, splashes, and spills.

There are no easy miracle cleaners, so the best course of action is to be very organized and disciplined.

stovetop habit

Get into the habit of wiping the stovetop clean immediately after use. A **damp cloth** should be enough but always finish with a **clean cloth** otherwise some food may be left behind, which will harden when the heat is on next. Avoid abrasive cleaners, and for hardened-on spills, squeeze on a spongeful of **warm sudsy water** or cover with a soaked cloth; leave for at least an hour before wiping off with a **clean cloth** or nylon scourer. Some fastidious fussers put **aluminum foil** underneath the burners where possible, but frankly it looks horrible and is an extravagant use of foil.

If, despite solicitous soaking and scrubbing, the marks persist, you may have to resort to a **commercial miracle cleaning spray**—and then resolve to develop the stovetop habit.

Oven Heaven

Wiping down the oven after each cooking session is, of course, the best way to keep it clean, but once the oven door is closed it's easy to forget about it. If done fairly frequently, it can be cleaned using **hot water** with a good squirt of **dishwashing liquid** and a **nylon scourer** (avoid steel wool as it scratches), resorting to a mildly abrasive cream for stubborn stuff. If you are a once-a-year oven cleaner, you will have to resort to **specialty oven cleaners** that are effective but highly toxic. Follow the instructions very carefully, wear rubber gloves, protect floors and other nearby surfaces, and make sure there is plenty of ventilation.

Clean dirty **oven shelves** by immersing in a mixture of 1 part washing soda (sodium carbonate) to 4 parts hot water.

To freshen up a **microwave**, place a few slices of lemon in a bowl of cold water, heat uncovered to boiling point on high, then cook on high for 60 seconds.

Refrigerators and Freezers

Refrigerators and freezers will work more efficiently if they are defrosted regularly. Don't forget to check the temperature—no warmer than 37°F for the refrigerator and 0°F for the freezer.

quick once over

• Sometimes it is only when you look closely at a neglected refrigerator that you see the finger marks on the outside and the drips and blobs of food on the inside. Keep things fresh with a regular clean.

• Take out all shelves, drawers, and removable storage parts before washing.

• Wash down the outside and inside using a cloth and warm water with a small squirt of dishwashing liquid. Pay attention to the outlet pipe, which may have gathered gunge and become partially blocked; pop in a little baking soda to help wash it out.

• Wipe off the shelves with a cloth or, if they are very dirty, wash them in a sink full of sudsy water.

- Finish the inside by wiping down with a weak vinegar and water solution, which will freshen the atmosphere.
- Dry everything thoroughly using a soft, dry cloth.
- If possible, pull the refrigerator away from the wall and remove the dust on the metal grille using a vacuum cleaner or damp cloth.
- Clean out the drip tray—soak up the water and any moldy drips with a cloth or paper towels, wipe clean, and dry thoroughly.

Don't bother with expensive
refrigerator deodorizers; a small bowl
of baking soda in the refrigerator
will absorb any strong smells.

Countertop Appliances

To clean **food mixers and blenders** after use, add 1 teaspoon dishwashing liquid to ¾ cup of warm water and whizz for 30 seconds.

Crumbs left in a **toaster** will burn and taint the toast. Unplug the toaster, empty the crumb tray or, if there isn't one, hold the toaster upside-down over a trash container and tap it to get everything out. Use a small pastry brush or soft toothbrush to gently brush debris off the elements.

When grinding coffee beans, there is always a little left behind in a **coffee grinder**. Over time it will become stale and taint any new coffee. Use an artist's brush to remove it, but unplug the appliance first.

To clean electric (or stovetop) **kettles**, pour in ½–¾ cup vinegar and an equal amount of water, then bring to a boil, leave overnight, and rinse.

Dishwasher Discipline

Dishwashers are great. They keep the kitchen tidy and get things a lot cleaner than most humans. And the good news for eco-warriors is that they are not as wasteful on water as you might expect. They work well if you follow the manufacturer's instructions, but it is surprising how dirty they can get. Empty and clean the filters regularly and give door seals a regular wipe down with warm sudsy water. If you live in a hard water area, make sure the salt reservoir is regularly topped up.

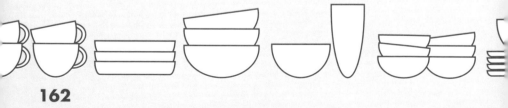

• To **freshen up** the dishwasher, place a shallow bowl of vinegar ($\frac{2}{3}$–$\frac{3}{4}$ cup) in the bottom rack and run a full wash cycle.

• To remove **milky film** from glassware, put a bowl filled with vinegar in the bottom of the dishwasher and run an entire cycle.

• Treat **odors** by sprinkling borax in the bottom and leave overnight, then wipe down the inside. There is no need to rinse, just do the next load.

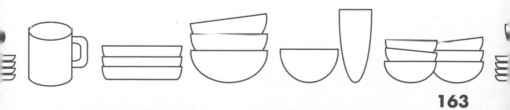

Washing Machines

The washing machine is a wonderful invention and deserves to be looked after.

The **detergent dispenser** gets clogged up, so take it out, immerse it in hot sudsy water, and scrub it clean. Use a toothbrush to get into the corners.

Before putting it back in, clean the **detergent dispenser's space**. You may be horrified to see how much sticky detergent and softener has accumulated. New soap powders, tablets, and liquids are formulated for use at low temperatures. While this is good for energy conservation and fabrics, the water is not hot enough to kill a number of **bacteria and molds**, resulting in a smelly washing machine. To cure this, do a 195°F wash at least once a month.

Limescale buildup damages the machine as well as impairing performance (see page 118). If hard water is a problem, use commercial water softeners that can be used with each wash or use a stronger limescale remover at regular intervals.

10 Laundry List

How often you change the bed linen depends on your standards and circumstances, but even if you sleep alone and always bathe or shower before bed remember all those dead skin cells and sweat—and even prim and proper people dribble in their sleep.

Soap Opera

The good news is that modern detergents are so efficient that, provided you follow the instructions, they even remove what used to be regarded as "stubborn stains."

They come in powder, concentrated powder, tablet, and liquid form, and your choice depends on the state of the laundry, personal preference, and what works best in your machine.

• **Biological detergents** contain enzymes, which break down dirt and make a meal of stains. However, they also contain chemicals that can provoke allergic reactions and skin irritations.
• **Non-bio** alternatives are less harsh and kinder to the skin but less effective on super stains.
• **Eco-friendly** detergents are kind to people, the planet, and your laundry, but are not always that good at tackling tough dirt and stains.

soft options

The world of fabric softeners can be a confusing one but their primary function is to soften fibers and remove any detergent residue. Many contain a cocktail of chemicals and artificial perfumes, so if you don't want that kind of thing stick to the eco-versions. Alternatively, add a couple of tablespoons of white vinegar to the final rinse.

CONTAMINATION ALERT!

If, despite your best efforts, a rogue black sock or green T-shirt has tinted and tainted your whites, remove the offending article and wash the load again (and again if the damage is great) using a biological detergent. If the problem persists, try using a powdered laundry bleach in with the load or soaking in mild bleach or a specialty commercial product. The bleaching effects of sunshine can also help.

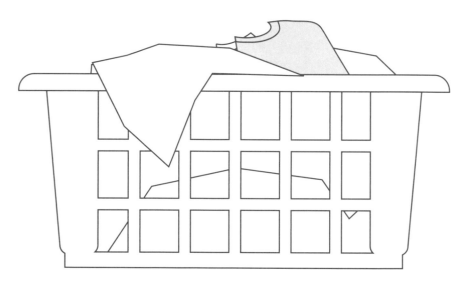

Washing Instructions

- **Read** each garment's label and follow the recommended washing instructions.
- **Measure** the laundry detergent and softener and use as directed.
- **Sort** your laundry into piles according to color, temperature, and fabric type.
- **Keep** whites white by washing in a whites-only load.
- **Don't overload** the machine and make sure that items are loaded loosely and not bundled together.
- **Do a smaller load** if the laundry is very dirty to allow room for agitation.
- **Use more detergent** in hard-water areas if necessary—see the detergent label for details.
- **Fasten** snaps, ties, and buttons on comforter covers to stop other items getting inside and forming a ball that will send your washing machine into a noisy spin.
- **Minimize** any irritating effects of a biological laundry detergent by running an extra rinse.

Dry Conditions

Clothes dryers are useful, especially if you have nowhere to hang things out to dry. However, they are expensive to run and the heat and tumbling can damage fabrics and reduce their life expectancy. Whatever drying method you use, always shake out or pull items into shape, especially along seams and embroidered sections to make ironing easier. Don't pull too hard as you could break the stitching.

outdoors

A long, **single clothesline** is best, but if space is restricted, a **rotary clothesline** is fine although items hanging on the inside will not dry so quickly.

Use a **plastic clothesline**, and before using clean it by running a damp cloth along it.

Hang **sheets** up by the hems rather than draping them over the line—they will dry more quickly.

Sunshine fades **bright colors**, so unless you want the shabby-chic look dry away from direct sun.

indoors

When drying clothes indoors, avoid creating **damp problems** by ensuring the drying area is well ventilated. By an open window or sunny spot is best.

There is a huge variety of **clothes airers** on the market and the choice depends on cost, space, looks, and personal preference, but avoid untreated wooden racks because they can stain the laundry.

Avoid folding items and **overcrowding racks** since things will take longer to dry and may become smelly. Rails that hook over radiators provide extra, quick-drying space.

The old-fashioned clothes airers that hang from ceilings look great and make the most of heat rising, but bear in mind that if you put one in the **kitchen**, the laundry will absorb cooking smells.

Drying Tips

• Remove any fluff from the dryer's filter either before or after every use.

• Make sure the dryer is vented as instructed by the manufacturer because the moisture can cause damp problems in your home.

• Don't overload since this leads to uneven drying.

• Don't mix different fibers as some dry quicker than others.

• Don't overdry items because it makes them more difficult to iron.

• Get rid of any hairs and bits of tissues stuck to laundry by tumble drying the affected items for 10 minutes on a cool setting.

• Make things smell nice by putting a handkerchief sprinkled with your favorite essential oil or perfume in with the load.

Between the Sheets

The smell and feel of clean sheets is one of life's little pleasures, and if you need an excuse, or a prod, to change the bed, here are a few facts and fixes.

• Eschew "easy-care" synthetic fibers. You can't beat **pure cotton or linen** for comfort.

• You can **save on washing** by changing just the bottom bed sheet and pillowcases and turning the down comforter over.

• Even if you aren't changing all the bed linen, **clean pillowcases** will feel good.

• **Use a flat sheet**, which is less bulky to wash, between you and the covered down comforter.

• Turn flat bottom sheets into fitted sheets by **tying a knot** in each corner.

• Change all bed linen after any illness. To kill any bugs, **wash at minimum 130°F** and iron on a high temperature.

• If you have an infection or are fighting spots with medication, **change your pillowcase** frequently to avoid any remaining bacteria causing reinfection.

Drapes and Covers

Because laundering is more thorough and involves fewer chemicals than dry cleaning (and is a lot cheaper), it's a good idea wherever possible to opt for machine-washable curtains and draperies, throw-pillow covers, blankets, and throws. Washing reduces the damaging effects of dirt and dust, but these items don't need laundrying very often, especially if you shake the dust out or vacuum frequently. Allow plenty of room for these bulky items to slosh around in the suds, do small loads, and if necessary use an extra-large machine at the laundrette. Use a cool wash cycle and use a dryer wtih a cool cycle and plenty of room, otherwise items will crease and might shrink.

quick freshen-up

• Vacuum curtains and drapes to keep down the dust.

• Give curtains and drapes a few hours outside on a breezy, sunny day.

• Hang curtains and drapes in a steamy atmosphere— just after your bath or shower; this freshens them up and is very good for perking up velvet.

• Put them in the dryer with a few fabric softener sheets for the cool 10 minutes at the end of a cycle.

Fabric Stains

The wonders of new detergents mean that a lot of stains that would previously have needed special attention magically disappear in the wash. The more stubborn varieties of stains may need **several washes** or a **pre-soak** in a solution of laundry detergent (make sure the detergent has fully dissolved) or an application of **neat detergent** on the affected area. Even if you don't use it normally, keep some biological laundry detergent ready for emergencies. Treatment will be more effective if you take **immediate action** to dilute the stain with water—preferably with bubbles.

stain reaction

- **tea and coffee**—rinse out the worst and wash immediately
- **red wine**—dilute with white wine or water and wash as soon as possible
- **blood**—apply neat biological laundry detergent and leave for a while before washing
- **red fruit**—if you have a steady hand, stretch the

stained area over a bucket or bowl and pour on boiling water from a great height, then soak in 1 part vinegar to 2 parts water. Otherwise use biological detergent and hope it fades over time.

• **curry**—the yellow turmeric stain (the main culprit) can be treated by rubbing with denaturated alcohol on a clean cloth before washing. It may take some time to fade but exposure to sunlight will help.

• **lipstick**—if bio-detergent doesn't work, use a proprietry stain remover

• **wax**—put the item in the freezer overnight (for big items put a freezer pack on the affected part). Chip off excess wax then place the fabric (wax side down) between two pieces of paper towel and apply a warm iron. If some wax remains, rub in a little vegetable oil, allow to sit for 10–15 minutes, and blot before washing.

try not to rub stains too much as it pushes
the stain farther into the fabric

182

Delicates Operation

When washing delicate fabrics use a gentle detergent, either an eco-variety or a product specially formulated for delicates. Washing by hand may be best but a machine wash is more thorough. Use a gentle, low-temperature program and place small, more fragile items inside a pillowcase.

Old cottons and linens can be whitened by soaking in a mild bleach solution although they will usually whiten with frequent washing. Follow the same procedure for mildew stains or soak in a bucket with two denture tablets. Remember that sunlight is also an effective bleach and stain remover.

Getting Steamed Up

5 good reasons for doing the ironing

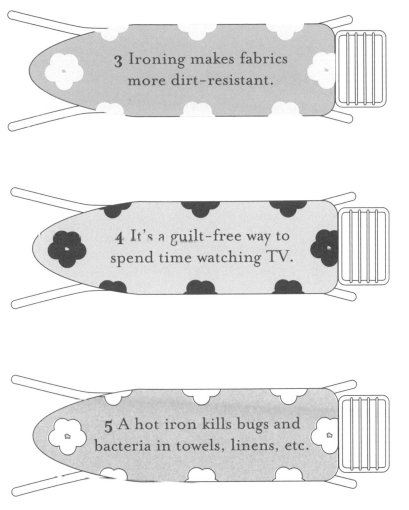

3 Ironing makes fabrics more dirt-resistant.

4 It's a guilt-free way to spend time watching TV.

5 A hot iron kills bugs and bacteria in towels, linens, etc.

Tips for Iron Maidens

• **Gently pulling** into shape and **neatly folding** dry laundry minimizes creasing and makes ironing easier.

• **Folding sheets** and large tablecloths double makes them easier to handle. Iron one side, fold with the pressed side on the inside and continue ironing and folding until you have a neat, folded, fully ironed item.

• Keep large items **off the floor** by draping the ironed bit over the back of a chair positioned behind the ironing board.

• Using **distilled water** in a steam iron prevents the buildup of limescale. Alternatively, use filtered water from a **filter pitcher**.

• **Descale** a steam iron by filling with a solution of 1 part water to 1 part vinegar. Steam for a few minutes, allow to cool, then rinse with clear water.

• Prolong the life of a new **ironing board cover** by liberally spraying it with **spray starch** then ironing it with a hot iron.

- Clean the **base** of the iron with a damp cloth dipped in **baking soda**.
- Better results will be achieved if you **iron things while damp**. If you are not going to iron right away, put them in a plastic bag in the refrigerator to stop them from becoming smelly.
- **Linen sprays** make ironing a more pleasurable experience. If you can't afford the posh versions, make your own by adding a few drops of lavender oil or another favorite essential oil to a spray bottle filled with water.

If you hate ironing, follow the fashion for shabby chic where creases are de rigueur. It's not the end of the world if your sheets are un-ironed. When bed linens are dry, pull into shape, fold carefully, and place at the bottom of the linen pile to flatten them.

Air Time

There was a time when if you went to bed in un-aired bedclothes you were thought to be putting your life in danger. Nowadays we tend not to think about such things, but while not exactly life-threatening, damp bedclothes are to be avoided. Items that have been steam-ironed require airing before use, so if you only have one set of sheets, try to wash, dry, and iron them in the morning to allow for airing time—or save up for a second set.

Air clothes on a clothes airer in a warm dry place, hang items over a radiator rail, or place on a sunny windowsill for at least an hour, preferably more.

put it away

The ideal of impressive quantities of perfectly folded, color coordinated linens and towels neatly stacked inside an equally impressive large linen cupboard or closet and topped with bunches of freshly picked lavender is seductive if not always achievable. You may not have such illustrious facilities but a drawer or shelf in the closet will suffice as long as it is dry. Alternatively, what about a wooden chest or a wicker basket? And don't forget the lavender.

• White bed linen and towels can turn **yellowy** over time, so if you are lucky enough to have piles of them, make sure you **rotate** them by always putting the clean ones at the bottom.

• Line drawers with paper—treat yourself to scented drawer liners otherwise use brown paper or wallpaper sprayed with essential oils, bunches of lavender and herbs, or leave old perfume bottles between the sheets.

Laundry List

189

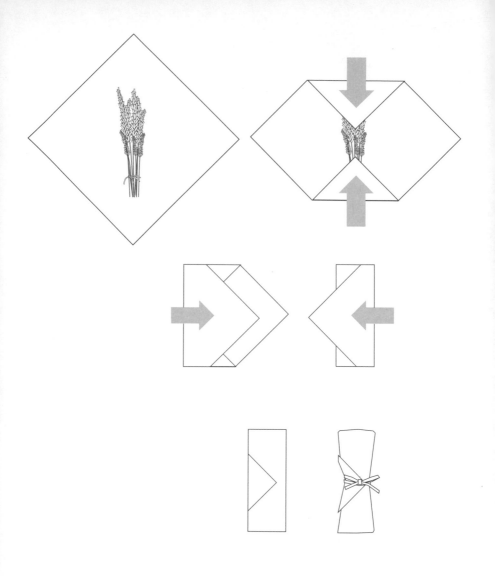

Pretty Pastime

With lavender and herbs growing in nearly every trendy garden, don't let them go to waste. If you fancy sewing lavender bags and herb sachets, go ahead. But if you are not nifty with a needle, wrap them up and tie with ribbon, string, or even a rubber band. Use fine muslin, which lets the smell out but stops the herbs from shedding and prevents possible staining. As a change from lavender, use cloves, cinnamon sticks, and orange peel.

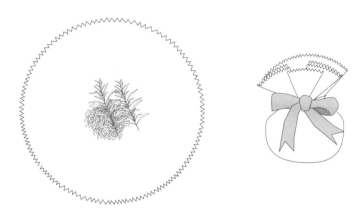

II Flawless Floors

A dirty floor makes your whole home look dirty even if it isn't. Neglecting floors is a little like spoiling a smart outfit by wearing worn-out shoes.

Carpet Care

Clean carpets are great. Those covered in bits and fluff detract from even the most stunning decor, and dirty ones just look disgusting. All carpets and rugs will benefit from regular attention.

- **vacuum** once or twice a week
- **mop up** any spills immediately
- **place** doormats at entrances to prevent shoes from tracking dirt into the house

Follow the manufacturer's instructions for special weaves and fibers, and don't use a rotating brush on natural floorcoverings such as sisal and seagrass because this will destroy the surface fibers.

quick carpet spring clean

1 **Remove** as much of the furniture as possible.
2 **Vacuum** the carpet thoroughly paying attention to edges and corners.
3 **Tackle** any obvious marks using a clean cloth wrung out in warm water with a squirt of dishawashing soap in it, or a suitable solvent for bad stains.
4 **Repeat** using clean water.
5 **Allow** to dry (you may want to leave the washed patches for a day to make sure they are thoroughly dry).
5 **Sprinkle** a proprietary dry powder shampoo generously all over the carpet.
6 **Brush** the powder into the pile using a clean stiff brush.
7 **Leave** for the length of time recommended on the instructions.
8 **Vacuum** thoroughly.
9 **Use** a stiff brush to raise the pile (optional).

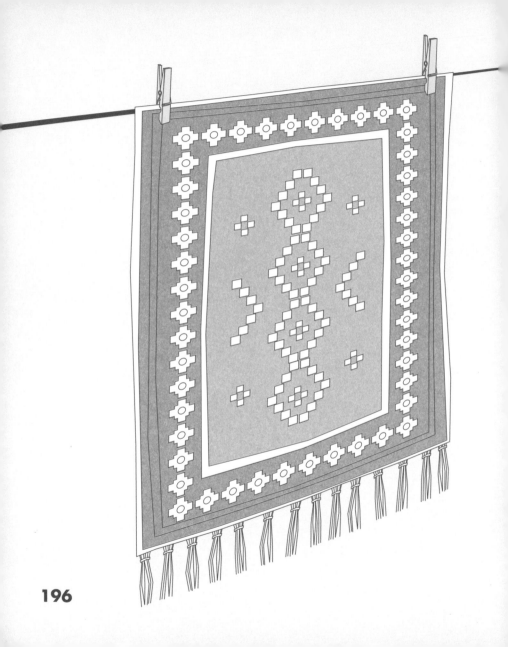

Beat That

A good bashing is brilliant for getting the dust out of rugs, kilims, and dhurries. Hang them over a clothesline or pole (but make sure it is up to the job) and beat them using a carpet beater (if you can find one) or a broom.

The rugs (and you) will enjoy it.

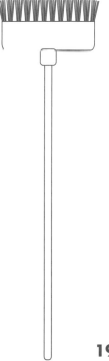

Carpet Stains

mild solution

A lot of carpet stains can be removed quite successfully if they are treated immediately with the stain emergency routine: blotting, diluting, washing with a mild detergent solution followed by rinsing with clean water and lots of blotting dry using clean, dry cloths. Spills of coffee and tea, white wine, blood, food (except curry), cola, and other sodas should respond well to this treatment as long as it is done promptly, but others may require something stronger.

stronger solutions

• **vinegar**—1 part vinegar to 3 parts water; apply with a sponge or cloth

• **mineral spirits**—use neat on a clean cloth

• **commercial carpet stain remover**—read and follow the instructions carefully; apply on a clean cloth or a spare sample piece of the carpet

When you have
new carpet fitted
keep a piece and
cut small sections
for testing any
stain remover before
applying. Solvents
often remove color,
and using a piece
of the same color
carpet will minimize
color loss.

stronger methods

Follow the mild solution with further action:

• **chocolate**, **ketchup**, and **red fruit** stains may
need a specialist stain remover
• **red wine**—don't put salt on it, blot instead with
white wine or water, followed, if necessary, by stain
remover
• **grease**—try the vinegar solution or mineral spirits
• **glue** and **solvent-based paint**—mineral spirits on
a piece of carpet or dry cloth
• **oil** and **tar**—dissolve and remove using eucalyptus
oil on a clean cloth followed by the mild solution
treatment
• **vomit**—mop or scrape up (a cake slice is useful) as
quickly as possible since stomach acids damage and
bleach out color; if the mild solution doesn't work,
try vinegar or stain remover
• **chewing gum**—harden using a freezer pack then
chip off; if that doesn't work, soften the gum with a
little petroleum jelly and ease it off the fibers using
your fingers

- **wax**—harden and chip off surplus wax using a freezer pack as for gum, then remove any remaining wax using brown paper or paper towels and a warm iron (a small travel iron is ideal), taking care to use a large enough area of paper to prevent accidently burning the carpet
- **trodden-in dirt**—this often looks much worse than it is; allow it to dry, vacuum up, then use further stain-removal treatment as necessary
- **dirt on sisal**, **jute**, and **seagrass**—blot up any spills immediately and treat serious stains with specialty products as recommended by the manufacturer; a cocktail stick is useful for digging out bits of spilt food or dirt
- **scorch marks**—difficult to remedy but trimming the damaged ends with scissors will make them less noticeable

Bare Essentials

Looking after bare floors is relatively simple and straightforward, especially if you follow a simple, regular routine.

sweeping

Dust may look harmless but it usually contains grit that gets ground into the floor and damages the surface. It's important, therefore, to clean floors regularly even if it's just a quick sweep. Use a fine, soft-bristled broom and/or a dustpan and brush.

vacuuming

Vacuuming is a good way to clean bare floors but be careful—big pieces of dirt and grit may get caught under the cleaner and scratch the floor so use a soft brush floor attachment. Use the thin, pointy attachment to clean corners, gaps, edges, and the tops of baseboards.

wet mopping

Most hard floors can be cleaned by mopping with warm, sudsy water as long as you are careful not to overwet the floor. Vinyl, linoleum, stone, tiles, laminates, and painted and solid wood can be mopped, but if you have an expensive new floor, follow the installer's instructions.

dry mopping and damp dusting

After a sweep, some floors, especially waxed ones, need only a quick buffing either with a dry duster tied around a dry mop or a slightly dampened duster.

Use wonder floor-treatments with caution because many leave residues that build up over time to form a dull, unattractive finish, which may also absorb extra dirt.

How to Mop a Floor

1 **Make** sure the mop and the bucket are clean.
2 **Fill** the bucket with warm water plus either a squirt of dishwashing soap or the prescribed amount of general-purpose surface or floor cleaner—make sure the water level is well below the compartment where you squeeze the mop.
3 **Dip** the mop in the water and squeeze out well; you don't want water sloshing around, especially on laminates where excess water can cause the surface to lift.
4 **Start** in one corner and mop the floor in front of you making sure you get into the corners and edges. On tiled floors don't forget the grouting between the tiles.

5 **Dip** and squeeze at regular intervals. Don't do too much with one mop-full, otherwise you will be spreading the dirt around rather than removing it.

6 **Change** the water in the bucket as soon as it looks obviously dirty.

7 **Empty** the bucket, rinse out, fill with clean, hot water, and rinse out the mop.

8 **Empty** the bucket again, refill with clean, warm water, and, squeezing as much water as possible out of the mop, go over the whole floor again—this may seem like hard work but you will be surprised to see how much more dirt you pick up.

School for Scrubbers

Getting down on your hands and knees to give the floor a good scrub can leave you, and the floor, remarkably refreshed. It's more thorough and can even be quicker and easier than mopping, especially in a confined space such as a bathroom or small kitchen.

1 **Pull** on your rubber gloves and get a kneeler—either purpose-made or a folded towel.

2 **Fill** a bucket with warm water and add a squirt of dishwashing liquid or all-purpose surface or floor cleaner.

3 **Dip** a large, absorbent cotton or linen cloth (or soft scrubbing brush) into the water, squeeze out, and start cleaning, rubbing briskly and paying attention to corners and edges and changing the water as soon as it gets very dirty.

4 **Tackle** tough dirt and hardened-on grime using a nylon scourer with neat cleaning product wherever necessary.

5 **Use** a scrubbing brush or toothbrush to clean the grouting between the tiles.

6 **Wipe** the just-cleaned section with the cloth squeezed out more thoroughly.

7 **Repeat** the process using clean warm water.

8 **Dry** off with a soft, absorbent cloth (you may need more than one).

Bare Facts

- **Waxed floors** look wonderful, but wax absorbs dirt and a buildup dulls the surface so apply wax only once or twice a year, depending on the amount of foot traffic. The same goes for **oiled finishes**.
- Never put wax on **varnished or laminate finishes** because it won't be absorbed.
- Remove **marks and scuffs** with a damp cloth and a little baking soda or liquid cleaner.
- Use very fine steel wool to tackle ingrained **dirt and scratches** on **wood or stone floors**.
- Soft stones, such as **limestone and marble**, are mostly calcium, which is soluble in acid, so don't use harsh cleaners. Use a mild detergent solution and avoid soap products as they form a scummy layer.
- Scrape off **chewing gum** with a palette knife and rub off the residue with fine steel wool.

interesting fact

Stone is soft when dug out of the ground, but hardens on exposure to air and foot traffic and forms a hard, self-cleaning surface over time.

safety alert

Shiny floors may look wonderful
but they can be treacherously slippery
to even the most sure-footed and
sober soul.

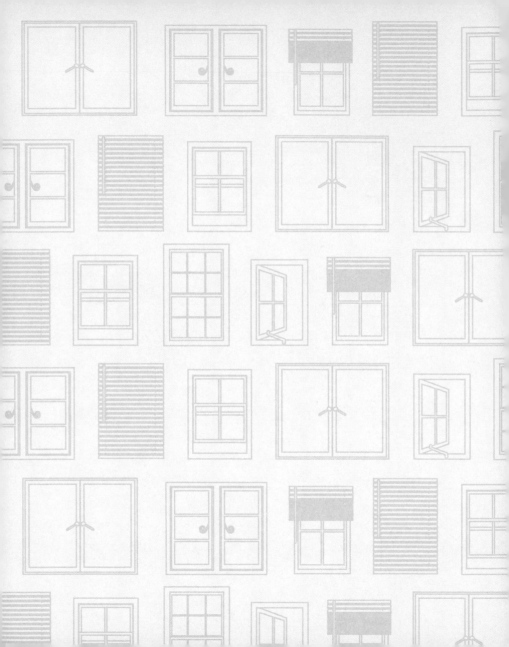

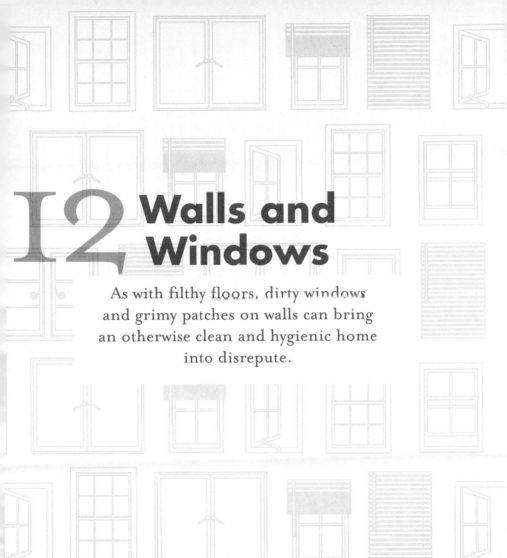

12 Walls and Windows

As with filthy floors, dirty windows and grimy patches on walls can bring an otherwise clean and hygienic home into disrepute.

When You're Cleaning Windows

Forget special window-cleaning products and newspaper soaked in vinegar—the best way to clean windows is with a mild detergent solution. Windows will only look really clean if they are done inside and out, but be careful if you are climbing on ladders or windowsills. Safety is more important than cleanliness, so it is far better to pay your friendly neighborhood window cleaner to reach the windows the safety-conscious occupant cannot reach.

- Put the sudsy solution in a spray bottle—it's easier to handle than a bucket.

- Don't wash windows on sunny days; they dry too quickly and streak.

- Wipe up and down on one side and side to side on the other so that when, inevitably, you spot a few streaks you know whether they are on the inside or outside.

one way for windows

- **Place** a towel or absorbent cloth on the windowsill to protect the paintwork from water.
- **Start** at the top and apply sudsy water (warm water plus a squirt of dishwashing liquid) with a cloth or nonscratch sponge scourer making sure you get into the corners.
- **Wipe** off any surplus with a wrung-out cloth.
- **Repeat** using clean water.
- **Dry** and buff with a soft, lint-free cloth.

another way for windows
• **Apply** sudsy water as before, then finish with a
window-cleaning squeegee.
• **Remember** to start at the top, don't forget the
corners, and have a dry cloth handy to wipe up the
drips from the squeegee.

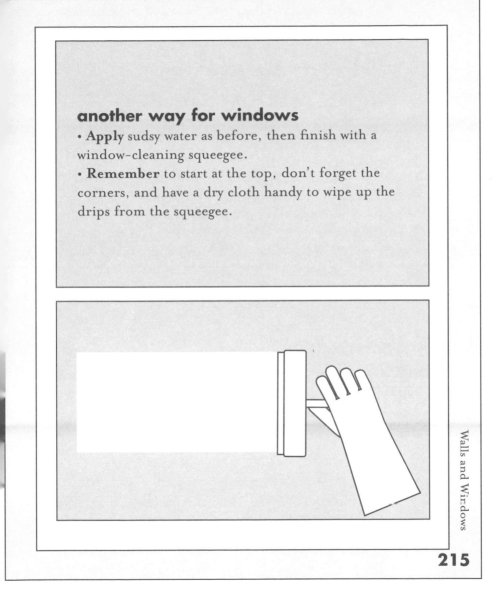

Blinding Light

5 ways to clean a venetian blind

with gloves
Dust the slats by hand wearing cotton household gloves. Brush off the dust as you go. For more neglected blinds, dip your gloved hands into a mild detergent solution, squeeze out excess water, and clean.

special implement
There are many specialty gadgets, and some of them ingeniously allow you to clean several slats at once. As with gloves, shake dust off frequently and wash after use.

hair dryer or vacuum cleaner
A quick blast with the hair dryer can dislodge light coverings of dust. But don't forget to collect the dust from that has settled on the floor. Alternatively, use a vacuum cleaner with an appropriate attachment.

bathroom

Clean plastic or metal blinds in the bathroom using the shower attachment. A few squirts of spray cleaner helps cut through grease. Alternatively, hang outside on the clothesline and use the garden hose.

on the floor

If it is easy to take down and you have enough room, spread out the blind on the floor with the slats closed. Clean using a duster, vacuum cleaner, or damp cloth (or all three). Turn over and clean the other side.

roller shades

If you have wipe-clean roller shades, then go ahead and wipe them clean using a damp cloth and, if necessary, a little mild detergent. For fabric blinds, dust regularly and thoroughly using a duster or vacuum cleaner. Most roller shades are treated to make the fabric stiffer so tackle stains with care. Try the gentle water and detergent method of removal, but follow the manufacturer's instructions and when in doubt use a proprietary stain remover.

Walls and Windows

Extra-Mural Studies

It is surprising how much dust settles on **walls**. Remove it using a long-handled feather duster or brush, or with a broom or dry mop with a clean duster tied around the head.

Wash **paintwork** on doors, door and window frames, baseboards, and picture or dado rails with a cloth or sponge and a mild detergent solution. Don't use anything stronger and don't use scourers since this will destroy the surface and make it less dirt resistant. Afterward, dry thoroughly.

Wash **dirty patches** with a damp cloth wrung out in a warm, weak detergent solution. Don't rub too hard because this will remove the paint. Use a paste or solution of baking soda for stubborn and greasy stains.

Freshen up **stained areas** behind work surfaces, sinks, stoves, and bedheads by washing down then repainting with watered-down paint (1 part paint to 2 parts water). It may be necessary to do the whole wall, otherwise it could look patchy.

If **damp and mildew stains** defy your attempts to remove them, paint the wall with a proprietary sealant or primer and then repaint.

If budding young artists have been **drawing on walls**, a soft eraser is the obvious choice to remove pencil marks.

For **crayon marks**, try covering the crayon with a baking-soda solution (or a lubricant spray, such as WD-40™) on a cloth, wipe off, and wash the area with warm sudsy water.

Wallpaper

Whereas paintwork can be washed, wallpaper needs gentler treatment. Clean **washable wallpapers** with a **damp cloth** but remember to follow the manufacturer's instructions.

Remove **dirty marks** on wallpapers with **white bread** gently squeezed into a ball. You can also use an **eraser**—the art-gum type is best because it crumbles as you use it and doesn't smear.

Remove **grease spots** by ironing on top of **brown paper or paper towels** placed over the mark. You could also try dusting with **talcum powder**; leave for a couple of hours before brushing off with a soft brush.

Remove **adhesive tape** with a **warm iron**—not on steam!—which will soften the glue and allow you to peel the tape off.

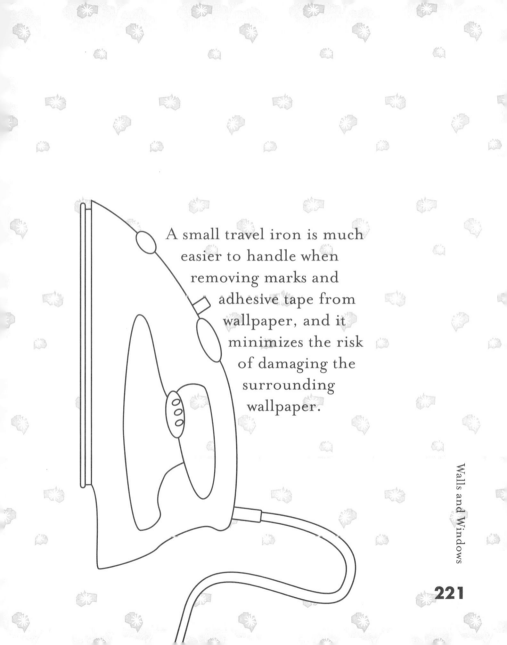

A small travel iron is much easier to handle when removing marks and adhesive tape from wallpaper, and it minimizes the risk of damaging the surrounding wallpaper.

Paper
Patchwork

Worn areas, tears, and bad stains can be repaired and hidden with a patch—providing you have some leftover wallpaper. Straight-cut edges will stand out, however, but torn edges will not, so tear out a piece slightly bigger than the damaged area—not forgetting to match up the pattern. Brush on some wallpaper paste, making sure the edges are well pasted. Place over the damaged area, slide into place to match the pattern, and smooth down, starting at the center, using a decorator's brush or soft dry cloth. If the color looks too new and bright, try "aging" the patch by dabbing with a damp cloth dipped in very weak tea or gently rubbing in a little dust from a duster.

13 Furniture Polish

Furnishings will look better and
last longer if you look after them.
Most care involves nothing more than
dust removal, an occasional wipe down,
and some buffing, but an accident or
serious case of neglect may require
a little more attention.

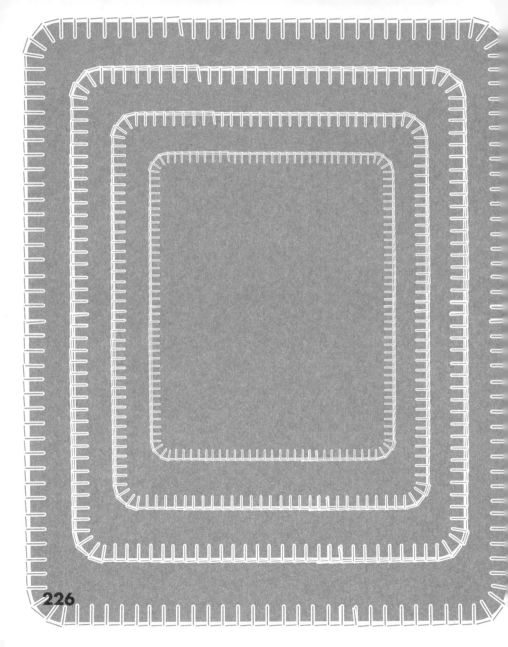

Buffer's Guide

Cleaning instructions often recommend a good buffing, a process that produces a satisfying glow on furniture, surfaces, and, if you work hard enough, your own face.

Proper buffing requires good lint-free cloths—linen or cotton, woven not knitted, and soft not scratchy— plus some elbow grease.

• First of all, remove any dust and surface dirt using a damp cloth.
• Allow everything to dry before rubbing briskly, making sure you get into every corner, nook, and cranny.
• For extra power, fold or gather the cloth so that it forms a small, thick wad enabling you to apply more concentrated pressure.
• When buffing wood, always go with the grain.

Wood Care

Wood matures, darkens, and mellows over time, especially if it is treated well.

varnished wood

Most new wood used in furniture is sealed with a varnish and therefore needs only a wipe over with the proverbial damp cloth and perhaps a small amount of detergent for sticky marks and dirt. Don't use a scourer or any abrasives because this will break down the surface allowing in dirt and moisture.

waxed wood

Dust regularly, wiping off dirt with a damp cloth. Wax once a year but don't put more wax on top of dirty wax—wax doesn't clean, it seals.

painted wood

Clean off marks with a damp cloth or wash with a mild detergent. Finish with a cloth squeezed out in clean water and dry thoroughly. Protect and bring a glow to nongloss paint finishes with an application of wax polish and buff well.

To remove a buildup of excess wax, rub with a solution of I part vinegar to I part water and dry immediately.

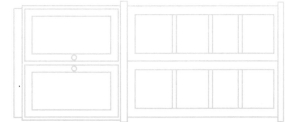

Furniture Polish

229

On Your Mark

- Put **petroleum jelly** on rings left by cups and glasses, leave for 24 hours, then wipe off.
- Use a small amount of **nongel toothpaste** on a clean cloth and rub until the mark has disappeared.
- Neat **liquid-cream metal polish** applied with a clean cloth should help remove any heat and water marks.
- Disguise scratches with **crayons**, **shoe polish**, or, on dark woods such as mahogany and cherry, **iodine**. Apply sparingly on a clean cloth or cotton wool.

New Lease of Life

Bring a glow back to tired, dry-looking, stripped pine or waxed wood with a wash and buff.

1 **Wash** with a damp cloth and warm water containing a little of dishwashing liquid, or with a proprietary wood wash). Use a nonscratch scourer on obvious dirt. Finish by wiping off with clean water.

2 **Wipe** off as much moisture as possible with a soft, lint-free cloth.

3 **Allow** to dry thoroughly.

4 **Apply** liquid wax or furniture oil with a soft cloth, applying evenly to avoid patches.

5 **Rub** off any surplus, following the instructions regarding drying time.

6 **Buff** vigorously.

smooth running

Cure squeaky hinges and loosen stiff catches with a squirt of fine spray oil, using the thin nozzle to get to the heart of the problem. If your drawers are sticking, rub the runners with the wax from a candle.

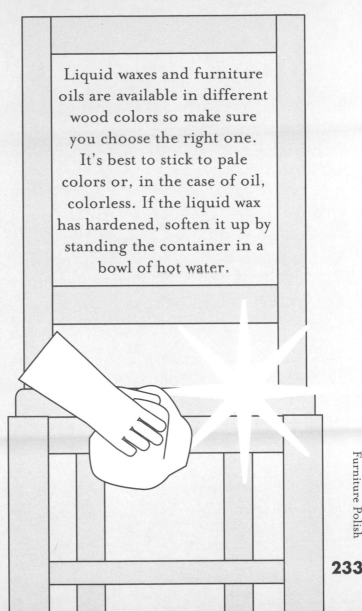

Liquid waxes and furniture oils are available in different wood colors so make sure you choose the right one. It's best to stick to pale colors or, in the case of oil, colorless. If the liquid wax has hardened, soften it up by standing the container in a bowl of hot water.

Leather

New leather furniture usually comes complete with the manufacturer's care instructions, so keep them in a safe place and follow them carefully. Don't get paranoid about a few marks and scratches, and accept that leather matures with use and acquires a patina that most people think improves both the look and the feel.

- If possible, keep leather out of **direct sunlight**, which dries it out and makes it crack. Dust frequently and unless otherwise instructed, clean off marks with a **damp cloth**.
- For **serious marks** on leather, wipe a cloth over a bar of **moisturising soap**, rub the leather clean, and then buff off.
- An occasional application of **hide food or saddle soap** will restore life and color. Do what it says on the label and buff well. If you are into shabby chic and love the look of old leather, even if it is torn and worn, this treatment will slow the process of deterioration.

Plastic Fantastic

Plastic and acrylic furniture looks good when new, but it is difficult to retain that shiny finish. Frequent dusting and buffing will minimize surface damage but accept that the surface will, in time, become softer, duller but more mellow.

Wipe down plastics and acrylics occasionally with a damp cloth, and for dirty marks, try a small amount of neat dishwashing liquid. Never use harsh abrasives or scourers.

For scratches on acrylics, try rubbing in a small amount of nongel toothpaste, buffing until the toothpaste, and hopefully the scratch, have disappeared.

Tabletop Tips

Glass tabletops are vulnerable to scratching so always use **tablecloths and mats**. Clean off smears and grease with a **damp cloth and sudsy water** and polish dry. Polishing with a little **denatured alcohol** on a clean cloth removes grease and retains sparkle. You can try removing scratches using **nongel toothpaste**. Chips can be filed down using a **fine emery paper**, but be careful not to damage the surrounding surface—or your fingers.

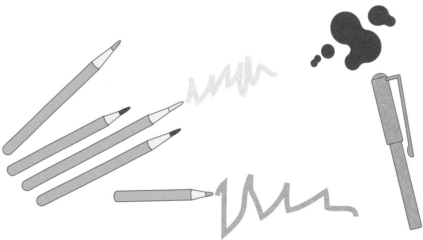

desktop polishing

Most of us now have a work area in our homes complete with home computer and related equipment. Keeping equipment on a **mat**—a place mat or small cotton dhurrie, depending on the size of the item—protects surfaces from damage and allows you to slide things around for cleaning.

A nonabrasive, **all-purpose surface cleaner** can remove **ink and felt-tipped pen marks** (but not indelible versions) from laminates or varnished wood.

Rubber-based **white glue** can be removed with **warm suds**; don't scour, just wait for it to dissolve.

Carefully scrape off blobs of **solvent-based glues** with a small paint scraper and dissolve any remaining residue with **mineral spirits or nail-polish remover** which is, of course, also the best thing for removing spilled **nail varnish**.

Upholstery

If your couches and armchairs are looking tired and dusty, perk them up with a little TLC.

fixed covers

1 **Take** off any loose seat and back cushions and plump them up.

2 **Vacuum** the cushions and frame using a brush attachment and the narrow nozzle tool to get down the sides and backs.

3 **Wipe** over with a barely damp cloth, wrung out in clean water.

4 **Tackle** stains with a cloth dampened in a solution of warm water and a squirt of dishwashing soap. Resort to a proprietary stain remover if necessary.

slip covers

• The great thing about slip covers is that they can be taken off and washed or dry-cleaned. However, getting them on and off can require a big effort, so if they are not too dirty, freshen them up as for fixed covers.

• If you do remove them, follow the manufacturer's washing or cleaning instructions carefully.

• Because covers are big and bulky it's best to wash them in a big machine at the launderette. When you take them out, pull them into shape and dry them naturally because using a dryer tends to shrink fabrics.

• The shapes can be awkward but ironing helps to keep the fabric clean, and if you are careful, you can always run the iron over them after they have been put back on.

Put slip covers back on while they are still slightly damp as they will shrink to fit.

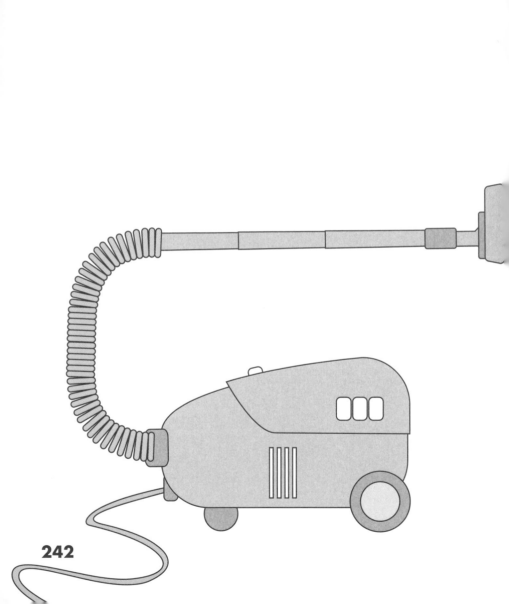

242

Feather Facts

• Plump up pillows by shaking to redistribute the filling and punching gently to get rid of dust.
• Don't plump them up too passionately because this can break the feathers.
• Putting feather pillows out in the sunshine helps to fluff up the feathers.
• Beware—strong suction vacuuming can suck the feathers out!

bed advice

Take your bed apart from time to time and dust the frame thoroughly. Use a vacuum cleaner to remove dust and detritus from the mattress (don't forget to do both sides), padded headboards, and box-spring bases. Turn the mattress over regularly according to the manufacturer's instructions.

Furniture Polish

Pro Antimacassar

How we laughed at dear old grandma's antimacassars—
lace-edged or embroidered—but today's heavy use of
hairwax and gels suddenly makes them seem like a
good idea again. Avoid embarassing stains and
protect the backs of your chairs and sofas.

5 alternative antimacassars

1 **cotton or wool throw**—folded for neatness

2 **cotton dhurries**—the washable kind

3 **cotton or linen tablecloth**—lots to choose from
and easy to launder

4 **extra-large napkins**—buy a dozen and change
them frequently

5 **lace or embroidered antique antimacassars**—
why ever not?

To keep wicker and rattan soft and prevent it from drying out, treat it with vegetable oil (not extra-virgin olive oil, sunflower oil is thinner and cheaper). Put it on sparingly with a soft brush, rub it in, and rub off any surplus with a soft cloth. Be careful to avoid surface oil on areas that come into contact with clothes. Warming the oil thins it down making it easier to apply.

Wicker and Rattan

Dust collects in the weaves of wicker and rattan and soon turns to dirt if not removed. Dust frequently using a soft brush or vacuum cleaner with brush attachment. If it is very grimy, wash with warm sudsy water, using a soft-bristled brush such as a toothbrush or dishwashing brush to get into the nooks and crannies. Remove as much moisture as possible with a soft, dry cloth and then allow to dry naturally.

14 Precious Possessions

Treasures and precious objects deserve to be looked after, but they often require extra care to preserve both their looks and value. For antiques and collectors' items, it is best to seek and follow expert advice either from dealers or specialty books.

Retro Perspective

That thrift store, garage sale, vintage, or retro bargain often needs a good clean. Don't get carried away, though, as overcleaning can destroy surfaces and character, and can even reduce the value.

• Old laminates are more more vulnerable to damage: the edge trims are glued on so they will peel off if water gets under them. They are also less heat-resistant so be sure to use mats and trivets.
• Do not use scourers or abrasives; clean with warm water and detergent and soften hardened-on dirt by soaking with a damp cloth. Pick out dirt from nooks with a cocktail stick rather than a sharp metal object.
• Wipe down leatherette and vinyl with a mild detergent and a damp cloth taking care to keep water out of seams, and dry thoroughly. As they are more prone to cracking and splitting, keep away from radiators, heaters, or bright sun.
• Clean metal trims, legs, and frames with the damp-cloth treatment. There is not much you can do about rust patches on chrome except carefully rub off any rough areas with a nonscratch scourer.

251

Antique Tips

When cleaning very expensive and valuable items, it is advisable to consult the experts, use specialty cleaning products, or get them professionally treated and cleaned.

In the meantime, keep them well buffed and dutifully dusted.

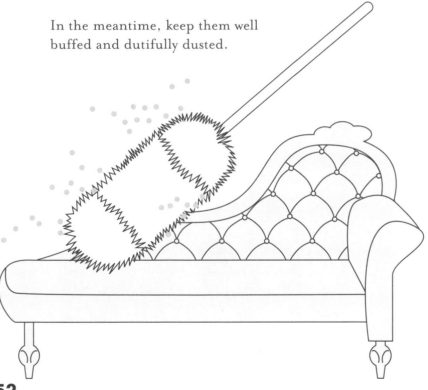

• Keep precious furniture out of strong sunlight, which fades wood and fabrics. If this is impossible, turn furniture occasionally to ensure even fading and close drapes at times of maximum sun.

• Don't place hot, cold, or wet objects directly on the surface. Use a mat.

• Heating systems dry the atmosphere causing cracking, loose joints, and warping. A humidifier maintains a constant level of humidity in the air, but placing a bowl of water in the room will also help prevent wood from drying out.

• For general cleaning, use a duster or barely damp cloth. Buff with a dry cloth to form a hard surface.

• Don't wax unnecessarily. Use a good-quality beeswax polish once or twice a year, polish sparingly, and preferably allow to dry overnight before buffing.

• Avoid aerosol spray polishes. They often contain silicon, which builds up a sticky surface, and a spirit, which removes natural oils in the wood.

• Don't clean metal handles with metallic cleaners as it will stain the surrounding wood; just buff them.

Exquisite Accessories

Treat antique glass with care and never put it in a dishwasher. Likewise, the glazes on older ceramics may not be very stable and are almost certainly not dishwasherproof. Instead, wash them in warm, mild suds using a sponge or soft cloth; never scrub and accept that some marks cannot be removed.

To remove **tea and coffee stains** from pots, put in a couple of heaped teaspoons (more for big pots and heavy staining) of **baking soda** and top up with **warm water**, leave overnight, and wash clean.

Clean vases, pitchers, and decanters in the same way. Use **vinegar** if something stronger is required—rub it on, or add water (I part vinegar to 2 parts water) and allow to soak. Alternatively, drop a **denture tablet** into a vase full of water and leave overnight.

hand wash with care

It's always best to wash precious items by hand. A plastic bowl has a soft surface, but washing directly in the sink gives more room for maneuver. Either way, put a cloth (one or two dishtowels or a terrycloth towel) in the bottom to protect against damage and breakages.

• Get rid of loose, surface dust before washing.
• Use a gentle, colorless dishwashing liquid.
• Wash in warm suds using a sponge or cloth and a soft brush, such as a blusher brush, to get into crevices and around handles. Do not rub too hard.
• Drain on a dish drainer or draining board lined with a towel or cloth.
• Leave to air dry or dry carefully with a clean, soft dishtowel or a hair dryer on a warm setting.
• Gently buff the surface with a soft cloth.

Silver Service

Solid silver is fairly soft so treat with care to avoid scratches. Silver-plate consists of a layer of silver on top of a more robust metal. While good-quality silver-plate has a relatively thick coating, inexpensive versions have a thin layer that gradually wears off. The best way to keep silver looking good is to use it. Wash it in warm sudsy water, rinse well, dry, and buff with a soft, lint-free cloth. Unused it will tarnish, unless stored away wrapped in acid-free tissue or nondyed cotton or linen, which seems a shame.

Tarnish is caused by humidity, so if you do keep it on display, choose a dry environment and dust regularly using a soft brush. Buffing quickly will deter tarnish buildup but it may be necessary to restore shine using a special silver cleaning product. As these products often remove a small amount of silver along with the tarnish it is best to eschew the liquid cleaners in favor of the impregnated cloths, which are gentler. For items with wooden knobs and handles, be careful to keep the cleaning materials off them because they can stain and damage the wood.

Bare hands and rubber
gloves will tarnish silver,
so wear cotton gloves when
dusting and cleaning.

stainless steel and aluminum

These metals should not require anything more than dusting and a wipe with a damp cloth from time to time. Small decorative items such as candlesticks or bowls and platters used for food should be washed in warm, sudsy water, rinsed, and dried thoroughly. If some staining does occur, try a paste of baking soda or use a special proprietary product.

plastics

Old plastics have become collectors' items, and although plastic will not rust or tarnish, it still needs to be cared for. The safest approach is to wipe down with a cloth dipped in mild detergent, rinse, and buff with a dry, soft cloth. Never use abrasives or scourers. Polish the surface and remove fine scratches with metal polish. Finish off with an antistatic cloth.

wall hangings and textiles

As ever, dust is the enemy so keep as dust-free as possible either by shaking gently, brushing with a soft-bristled brush, or using a vacuum cleaner on a low setting.

pictures and mirrors

• Don't hang valuable original pictures over a radiator or fireplace because the heat will damage them.
• Avoid damp walls and direct sunlight.
• Don't spray liquids directly onto glass as they can seep through to the picture or mirror and damage the frame or glass.
• Stop mirrors from steaming up in bathrooms by rubbing with dishwashing liquid and polishing with a clean soft cloth.

books

Hold precious books closed and brush the edges of pages using a big make-up powder or blusher brush.

15 Electrical Equipment

Static electricity turns electrical
equipment into a magnet for
dust, which not only looks unsightly
but can affect performance and
efficiency over time.

Lamps and Light Fixtures

Dust loves lamps and light fixtures where it often sits unnoticed. Don't forget to include fixtures, lamps, lampshades, and bases in your dusting routine.

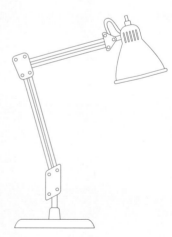

Don't forget to dust the light bulbs! The light will shine brighter.

For safety's sake, unplug lamps when cleaning and remove lampshades from central lighting.

Shady Business

• The material used for a lampshade is often **glued** to the metal frame therefore wetting is to be avoided.
• Hold **cardboard lampshades** by the metal frame and dust gently with a very soft duster, brush, or vacuum cleaner. Tackle dirty marks with an **eraser**, **white bread** rolled in a ball, or a **damp cloth**.
• Dust **fabric lampshades**, preferably with a vacuum cleaner, and use a proprietary spot cleaner on stains.
• Expensive **fabric lampshades** are sometimes sewn to the frame so they can be washed carefully in **warm sudsy water**. Rinse well—a gentle shower hose will force out more soap and dirt—shake off any excess water, and gently blot off as much moisture as possible using a clean, dry towel. Allow to dry, preferably in a sunny or breezy position.

• **Plastic lampshades** can be washed in **warm sudsy water**. Rinse, dry thoroughly, and finish by wiping with an antistatic cloth.

• Wash **glass lampshades** in **warm sudsy water**, rinse, and dry thoroughly.

• Dust **metal lampshades** and desk lamps thoroughly and then wipe off marks with a **damp cloth**; or for tougher dirt, rub with a cloth wrung out in **mild detergent** taking care not to splash any water into switches.

• **Chandeliers** will retain their sparkle if they are dusted frequently and occasionally washed in **warm sudsy water**. Wear **cotton gloves**; it's not only safer but keeps greasy finger marks off the glass.

Computers +

Computers, music systems, televisions, video players, and DVD players are often not the most attractive items and look even worse if they are dusty, discolored, and covered in finger marks.

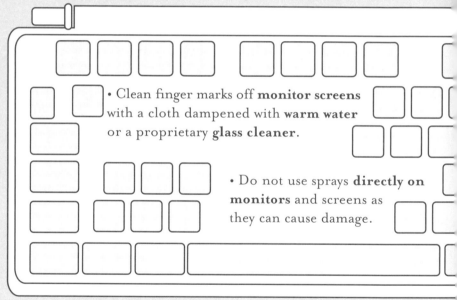

• Clean finger marks off **monitor screens** with a cloth dampened with **warm water** or a proprietary **glass cleaner**.

• Do not use sprays **directly on monitors** and screens as they can cause damage.

• Clean **casings** (not keyboards) with a **damp cloth**, using a little **denatured alcohol** on **discoloration**.

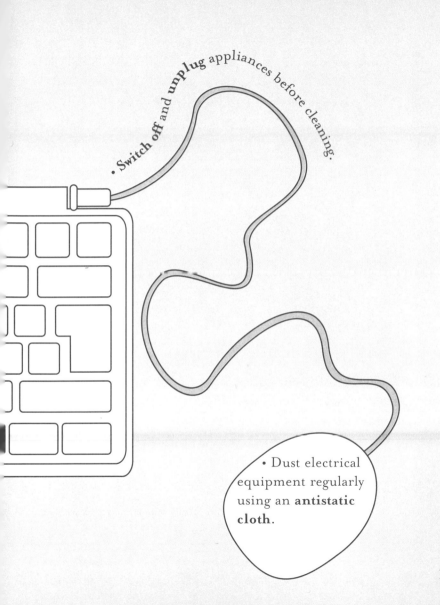

• Switch off and **unplug** appliances before cleaning.

• Dust electrical equipment regularly using an **antistatic cloth**.

Dust keyboards with a soft cloth, or feather duster, turn upside down to remove crumbs, and use a small artist's paintbrush (or a photographic lens brush with puffer) to remove remaining fluff. Don't be tempted to blow out the dust because the moisture in your breath could cause damage. If the brush doesn't get everything out, use a can of compressed air, available from electronic stores and departments. You could also use a vacuum cleaner if you have a suitably soft brush attachment and low suction setting, but read the manufacturer's instructions first.

Not only do computers and equipment attract dust, they are often not the most attractive items in a room, so why not make dustcovers to complement the decor? If you are a whizz with the sewing machine, make semi-fitted covers; otherwise, cover them with a small throw, attractive fabric, or a gorgeous shawl.

shock tactics

There are a number of commercial antistatic treatments around, but here is an inexpensive and cheerful alternative to make yourself.

1 Soak a lint-free cloth in fabric softener diluted with water.
2 Squeeze out any excess liquid and allow to dry before use.
3 Treat two or three cloths at a time to ensure a good supply.

16 Pets' Corner

If you have a pet, it is important to keep your home as clean, sweet-smelling, and allergen-free as possible. And the best place to start is with the animal concerned...

Pong Patrol

Animal owners love their pets, but they are often unaware that their homes smell distinctly doggy or decidedly catty. As well as good grooming and rigorous cleaning routines, make sure there is plenty of ventilation to maintain a fresh atmosphere. Use natural products to scent or deodorize the home, and don't use artificial air fresheners—even if they don't affect you, they may well harm your pet.

273

Good Grooming

- Regular grooming will not only make your pet less smelly but will also remove some of the dead skin and saliva flakes that cause allergies in humans.
- If possible, groom your pet outdoors so that the hairs and flakes are blown away rather than just redistributed in the home.
- It isn't advisable to bathe dogs more than once every 3 months because it can dry their skin and cause irritation. It isn't advisable to bathe cats at all for your own safety!
- Provide pet bedding that is washable and wash it frequently. Washing at 130°C will kill bugs and any eggs from fleas.

- Drying bedding in the clothes dryer will sterilize it and remove pet hairs.
- If you allow pets on furniture and beds, either protect them with a washable cover or wash the actual covers frequently.
- Vacuum and mop frequently around and underneath pet beds and their favorite places.
- A good vacuum cleaner will pick up most hairs from upholstery and carpets as long as you do it frequently, but a wiping it with a damp cloth may be more thorough.
- Blot up urine immediately. Rinse with a vinegar and water solution, blot, and dry.

Flea Pit

Fleas irritate pets. Not only do they carry potentially harmful diseases—the fleas on the rats actually carried the bubonic plague!—they cause itchy spots that can lead to serious skin problems. Fleas bite humans, too.

flea spotting

Fleas are dark brown and wriggle or jump, so look out for them when grooming your pets. They tend to live along the spine and around the neck, where you may also notice other small dark specks that are not flea eggs but droppings. If you manage to pick any fleas off your pet, put them in a bowl of water otherwise they will hop off (or back on).

animal treatment

The vet is the best person to give advice and treatment. There are several ways of getting rid of fleas on your pet, including sprays, powders, flea collars, tablets, and insecticidal liquids. Always follow the instructions carefully and don't use a product designed for one species on another—a dog product on a cat, for example.

home treatment

By treating your pet and your home, you will keep both free of fleas.

Wash your pet's bedding frequently. Unfortunately, fleas lay their eggs away from animals, so even if you rid the pet of fleas there are others hatching elsewhere ready to hop on and start all over again. Using a powder or spray at frequent intervals over a period of time will help break the cycle. Spray bedding, chair, and floor coverings concentrating along the edges of carpets and baseboards—and don't forget to put some in the vacuum cleaner bag. As with any insecticides these sprays and powders are potentially harmful if breathed in or ingested, so use carefully and follow the instructions. Tropical fish and small children are particularly vulnerable and any food should be covered to avoid contamination.

If problems persist and you suspect you have an infestation, call in the experts who will treat your home efficiently and safely.

Words on Worms

Even the best-loved and pampered pets can get worms, and as they can cause distress and ill-health they must be dealt with. There may be no obvious signs but look out for worms in their vomit, excrement, and around their nether regions. There are two kinds of worm: roundworm and tapeworm.

roundworms

Roundworms look like very thin, pale earthworms. They are spread from animal to animal, and can be passed on to humans if the eggs are accidentally ingested from the fingers, from plates that pets have licked, or from the soil.

tapeworms

A tapeworm is a long flat worm made up of segments, with a head that attaches itself to the intestine. Mature segments break away and can be seen in excrement or around the base of the tail; they look like grains of rice. Tapeworms in dogs are often spread by fleas and in cats by fleas, mice, shrews, and voles, but they can also be picked up from uncooked meat.

treatment

It is always best to consult a vet as he or she will offer professional advice and prescribe the correct dosage for your pet. Professionally administered or prescribed treatments tend to be more effective, but licensed roundworm and tapeworm remedies are also available from pet stores. Always follow the manufacturer's instructions and keep all medicines away from children.

Most worms will not usually affect humans, but there are a few that can cause severe illness so it makes sense to be vigilant and ensure that there are no traces of excrement in the house. Check your pet's bottom and the surrounding fur or hair regularly and be prepared to wipe or wash if necessary.

Clean out cat litter every day and be a good citizen and pick up and dispose of your dog's faeces so that no unsuspecting person or child will come into contact with it.

17

PS

Daily chores can be a bore, but traditional spring-cleaning will almost certainly raise your spirits and that of your home. You may find that reviving a tired-looking interior involves nothing more than a good dose of TLC. If, however, you are more desperate housewife than perfect homemaker, there is no shame in hiring someone to keep your home in the condition to which you wish to become accustomed.

Quick Transformation

Sometimes, people mistake the need for redecoration with the need for a good clean, so if redecorating doesn't fill you with enthusiasm or is just not an option, you can still transform a room using all the cleaning tips in this book plus a few changes.

clean

- clean windows inside and out
- get rid of dust from all surfaces including walls and window and door frames
- wash grubby paintwork and walls, and tackle stains and dirt around light switches, door handles, and baseboards
- wash work surfaces
- dust / wipe clean appliances
- dust / wipe clean electrical equipment
- dust window blinds and wash or wipe clean
- wash or freshen up drapes, slip covers, throws, throw pillow covers, etc.
- vacuum upholstery, and clean and freshen up as necessary
- vacuum floors thoroughly, including carpets and rugs
- freshen up carpeting if necessary
- mop or scrub floors

clean +

- change the furniture around
- paint one wall a trendy color
- put up new pictures
- change the throw-pillow covers

The Big Clean

A major clear-out and a clean-up is good for the soul, and most homes will benefit from such activities at least once or twice a year. Even if you are the dutiful housewife type, there will be some top shelf with a vestige of dirt, and if you are a slob this provides an opportunity to salvage your reputation.

The actual cleaning methods are much the same as for normal daily or weekly chores, but the big clean involves being much more thorough, getting underneath everything and into every nook, cranny, corner, and crevice.

be prepared
• **Set aside** plenty of time to do things properly. Two days is ideal—aim to start early the first morning and finish the following afternoon leaving the evening free for a celebratory meal in the newly pristine environment.

• **Send** children, cleanaphobic partners, pets, and lazy housemates to stay with relatives or friends in order to ensure that they don't get in the way, fall over things, or demand gourmet meals despite the fact that the kitchen has been turned upside down and the stove is in pieces.

• **Check** that you have ample supplies of cleaning materials, implements, cloths, and sponges.

• **Stock up** on plenty of big plastic trash bags for trash, recycling, and items for rummage sales.

• **Be aware** of health and safety and get in a good supply of rubber gloves (including heavy-duty ones) and face masks to protect from excess dust or cleaning sprays and fumes.

• **Protect** valuable items and floors with large dustcloths.

• **Test** your stepladder to make sure it is in good order and safe to use. You will need it to get to high shelves, light fixtures, and tops of cabinets.

• **Empty** the vacuum cleaner and make sure it is in good working condition.

• **Reward** yourself for your hard work with a plentiful supply of treats. This is an opportunity to indulge in naughty-but-nice stuff such as potato chips, cookies, chocolates, and cake.

Getting Help

If despite all efforts you can't, or won't, clean your home and as a result are losing face and friends, it's time to hire someone to do it for you. Cleaning is not just for Christmas, it's for life; but while some are born to clean, others have cleanliness thrust upon them. However, few would dispute the fact that a clean home is more pleasant to live in, so if cleaning is not for you, why not consider paying someone to do it for you?

287

The Search

Finding someone to come and work for you is not always easy. Personal recommendation is preferable so ask friends and neighbors first. If nothing turns up, try an agency or advertise in the local paper or in a store window—don't give your address, just a telephone number (preferably for a cell phone).

references
Request references from previous employers and don't be afraid to follow them up, anyone who is any good won't mind. In the case of written references a quick telephone call will confirm that they are genuine and weren't written with a loaded mop held to the writer's head.

interview
The chances are that someone who takes no pride whatsoever in their appearance is unlikely to care much about the appearance of your home, but it's not always the case. However, long painted nails suggest an unwillingness to work hard, and whereas

dirty nails may imply the opposite, they may also indicate a lack of attention to detail. Don't be afraid to use your gut instinct when judging potential applicants. Remember, you will be handing over your front-door key so trust is imperative.

Don't spring clean the house before interviewing a cleaner—it may make you feel good but it won't offer any insight into what the actual job entails.

The Good Employer

Take your new cleaner around the house, agree on a basic set of tasks, and, if necessary, establish whether he/she is willing to be flexible, for example tackling ironing one week or giving the spare room a good going over the next. Make clear any "house rules" or "no-go areas," not forgetting to explain the security and alarm systems.

Cleaners are easily offended, especially if they arrive to find "keep out" signs and padlocks on the cabinets, so if you have particularly valuable items lock them away discreetly.

If you own a lot of precious furniture and objects, either check that they know how to care for them properly (you don't want that Ming vase put in the dishwasher), or declare them off-limits with cleaning duties restricted to the basics.

Don't feel you have to clean before the cleaner comes but it is polite to tidy up—remember you are employing a cleaner not a lady's maid.

Be nice to your cleaner and always pay promptly. Establish boundaries early on. It's a good idea to forbid them bringing anyone else such as children or friends into the house, and don't give them free range of the refrigerator as you could come home to find your favorite chocolate or tonight's dinner gratefully consumed. It's best to leave a tray attractively laid out with tea and coffee-making facilities plus, to show your appreciation, a few delicious cookies.

Keep the relationship professional; cleaners can too easily become a best friend or a tyrant, neither of which is desirable. Remember, you are the boss. It's difficult to complain that the bathtub isn't clean if you've just shared your innermost secrets over coffee.

Keeping Your Cleaner Equipped

Once you have found your cleaner, you may be shocked when they demand a better class of vacuum cleaner and insist that you stock their favorite cleaning materials. However, be warned, baking soda and vinegar are rarely on their list, instead you may be asked to buy new (and expensive) wonder cleaning products—the type that can destroy surfaces, your health, and eventually the planet. So if you feel strongly about such things, you may have be prepared to compromise (with branded, basic, proprietary products) rather than risk losing a good cleaner.

useful addresses

general cleaning products and tools

Home Depot
www.homedepot.com

eco-friendly cleaning products

Earth Friendly Products
www.ecos.com

Eco Mall
www.ecomall.com/biz/cleaning.htm

Ecover
www.ecover.com/us/en/Products

Go-green.biz
www.go-green.biz

Greenfeet—The Planet's Homestore
http://store.greenfeet.com

organizations and advisory bodies

American Veterinary Medical Association
www.avma.org

Care2 Make a Difference: "Top Ten Eco-Friendly
Ways to Clean the House"
www.care2.com/channels/solutions/home/511

Good Housekeeping Institute
http://magazines.ivillage.com/goodhousekeeping

Greenpeace (The Chemical Home)
www.greenpeace.ca/e/resource/green/

US Department of Health and Human Services
www.hhs.gov

index

Index

acknowledgments

Thanks to the Quadrille team: Jane O'Shea, the enthusiastic editorial director; Lisa Pendreigh, the perfect editor; and Claire Peters, the adventurous designer.

304